TREASURES OF THE VATICAN

TREASURES
OF THE
VATICAN

ST PETER'S BASILICA
THE VATICAN MUSEUMS AND GALLERIES
THE TREASURE OF ST PETER'S
THE VATICAN GROTTOES AND NECROPOLIS
THE VATICAN PALACES

INTRODUCTION BY
DEOCLECIO REDIG DE CAMPOS
Curator of Medieval and Modern Art, Pontifical Museums and Galleries, Vatican City

TEXT BY
MAURIZIO CALVESI
of the University of Rome

PORTLAND HOUSE
NEW YORK

© 1986 by Editions d'Art Albert Skira S.A., Geneva, Switzerland

This edition published in 1987 by Portland House,
distributed by Crown Publishers, Inc.,
225 Park Avenue South, New York, New York 10003

Library of Congress Cataloging-in-Publication Data

Calvesi, Maurizio.
    Treasures of the Vatican.

    Reprint. Originally published: Geneva: Skira, c1962.
    Bibliography: p.
    1. Art—Vatican City.   I. Title.
N2940.C33   1987   708.5'634   86-21203
ISBN 0-517-62643-8

Printed and bound in Switzerland

h g f e d c b a

CONTENTS

DEOCLECIO REDIG DE CAMPOS

THE VATICAN
AND ITS MUSEUMS

Many may wonder why and how it is that in the course of the centuries the popes have come to accumulate the fabulous treasures of the Vatican Museums, in particular the rich collections of ancient and secular art. It may perhaps be supposed that, in their lavish patronage of the arts, the popes were merely indulging the expensive tastes of powerful sovereigns—tastes much like those of secular princes, and devoid of any higher justification. Yet, as a moment's reflection will show, their patronage of great artists has its justification and *raison d'être*. The Catholic (i.e. the universal) Church claims in fact to have its "distinctive note" in the very universality implied by its name, for its message is addressed to all men the world over. And the term "catholic," in the etymological sense, also applies to its doctrine, which embraces, *sub specie Dei*, all created things together with the human person in its composite integrity of body and soul, whose ordained development on the natural and the divine plane is willed by God. This is the reason why the Church honours and encourages art, the noblest among the faculties of the human mind; and this is one of the reasons why in Rome, in the residence of the popes themselves, the Vatican Museums have come into existence.

Nearly two thousand years have passed since its foundation, and in that time the Church's interest in the arts has taken various forms, following the historical vicissitudes of aesthetic thought, which only in recent times has achieved a greater degree of clarity and method. Greater than before certainly, but by no means complete, because in the last analysis an insight into the living essence of art is always to some extent a matter of intuition; and, even when that essence is recognized, it seems to elude an exact conceptual formulation.

Up to the time of the Renaissance, the Church concerned itself almost exclusively with sacred art—with an art, that is, intended to embellish the places and objects of worship, to illustrate the truths of the Faith, and to tell the story, so that even the illiterate might understand, of the events of the Bible and the miraculous lives of the Saints. Art in itself mattered little to the medieval clergy; what it required was a particular kind of art performing a useful function. And this is readily understandable when we remember how little importance was then attached to the figurative arts, which were regarded as mere handicrafts and accordingly had no place in the noble ranks of the "liberal arts" (which, however, included music because it is based on numerical relationships). Art, for the men of that period, included the trades of wool manufacturer and apothecary, on the same footing with those of the architect, the painter, the sculptor and the goldsmith. Nor was any distinction made between artist and craftsman, who, moreover, were almost always both at the same time, and with the same devoted care and skill designed cathedrals and palaces, ornamented chalices and paxes, painted altarpieces and marriage chests, creating in all humility the countless anonymous masterpieces that have come down to us from the Middle Ages, like pearls from the bottom of the sea.

This peculiar conception of art, so different from our own, also explains why the medieval Church, while it handed down through the monastic scriptoria so many of the literary, poetic, historical, legal and scientific works of Greco-Roman antiquity, showed so little regard for the remains of classical sculpture and even at times encouraged their destruction. The writings it handed down were works belonging to the liberal disciplines, to the aristocratic arts of the *trivium* and *quadrivium*, while sculpture was not only the humble product of manual labour but for the most part represented the "false and deceitful" gods of the shattered pagan world, and might therefore exert a baneful influence on the faith of an ignorant and superstitious people. It is true that not all the classical texts diligently copied in the monasteries had been written by authors who were, as Tertullian described Seneca, *naturaliter christiani*. But these precious manuscripts meant nothing to the illiterate, while the small body of scholars, mostly ecclesiastics, who had access to them found in their own theological convictions the antidote to the dangerous poisons of those pagan writings; they knew, moreover, how to make the best use of the ideas and teachings to be found in them, thus enriching Christian thought with the legacy of antiquity.

This deep-rooted aesthetic prejudice does not seem to have cramped or interfered with the development of the arts in the Middle Ages, but the low social standing to which artists were thereby condemned cannot have done much to inspire them in their work. This state of affairs was challenged and radically altered by the artists and scholars of the Quattrocento and Cinquecento, from Leon Battista Alberti to Benedetto Varchi, who claimed for the "arts of design" the dignity and mark formerly accorded to them by Pliny and other ancient authors. In their writings these Renaissance polemicists sought to show (in their zeal often exaggerating) that the proficient exercise of art demands a sum of intellectual and scientific knowledge—extending to such fields as history, geometry and mathematics—by no means inferior to that required, for example, in rhetoric and music; and that painting, sculpture and architecture were accordingly fully qualified to share the coveted title of "liberal arts." To their writings Raphael added the eloquent plea of his paintings in the Vatican Stanze, where he included portraits of Leonardo da Vinci, Michelangelo, Bramante, Sodoma and himself, in the guise of philosophers and scholars, among the illustrious figures gathered together in the *School of Athens.*

The empty disputes over the hierarchy of the arts and the relative "nobility" of each would only make us smile today—for the argument never went below the surface to the heart of the aesthetic problem—were it not for the fact that they are the outward sign of a renewal of interest in art for its own sake and, what is more, the sign of a fresh insight into its genuine essence. An insight still obscure and subconscious, however, not yet translatable into conceptual terms; already clearly revealed in the pages of Vasari and the letters of Aretino when they let themselves go, airing their views on painting and sculpture, as artists and art lovers, but almost wholly absent from their theoretical discussions. The attitude of Michelangelo seems to me typical in this respect. When asked by Varchi for his opinion as to which of the two, painting or sculpture, was the higher art, he sent him a rather testy and impatient answer, to the effect that at bottom they came to "the same thing"; then, feeling the futility of the whole argument, he added with inspired pragmatism: "Why not let them consort together in peace and leave these disputes be, for they take up more time than making the figures?"

The Renaissance way—so different from that of the Middle Ages—of seeing and responding to a work of art as something which, in itself, in its intrinsic aesthetic qualities, has its own justification, independent of any purpose it might serve, placed the arts and letters on the same plane and opened the first chapter in the history of the museum, that instrument of culture henceforth as indispensable as the library. For centuries ancient manuscripts had been collected; from now on ancient works of art also began to be collected. Pope Sixtus IV (1471-1484) not only housed the Vatican Library (founded by Nicholas V about the middle of the fifteenth century) in a magnificent building and opened its doors to scholars and students; at the same time, in the Campidoglio, he founded the first public museum of modern times. Meanwhile, in Florence, the Laurentian Library was founded and the collection of ancient marbles was being made that stood in the Medici Gardens (where Michelangelo studied as a boy and discovered himself to be a sculptor born). Pope Julius II (1503-1513), a nephew of Sixtus IV, opened the gardens of the Belvedere to artists; there stood the antique statues which went to form the nucleus of the present collections of the Vatican Museums. It may be of interest to tell in brief the story of the growth and enrichment of those museums from the Renaissance to the present day. Much of what follows is based on the facts gathered together, in their scholarly studies, by Ludwig von Pastor and Bartolomeo Nogara.

The small palace known as the Belvedere, built for Pope Innocent VIII about 1487 by Jacopo di Pietrasanta, to the designs of Antonio Pollaiolo, at first consisted of a single pavilion open on the north side and an east wing, added in the course of construction to the original building in order to give it the character of a modest summer palace. Between the two wings was a small garden in which Julius II placed an *Apollo*, thereafter known as the *Apollo Belvedere*, which he had acquired while still a cardinal and which, prior to his election, had stood in the palace adjoining his titular church of San Pietro in Vincoli. To this famous statue, believed at that time to be a Greek original, were added the following works during the decade of his reign (1503-1513): the *Laocoön* group unearthed in 1506 in the vineyard of Felice de' Freddi on the Esquiline and immediately purchased by the pope; the *Torso Belvedere* so much admired by Michelangelo; the *Venus Felix*; the *Sleeping Ariadne*, then believed to represent Cleopatra and as such celebrated by Castiglione in a famous Latin poem; the *Meleager*; the recumbent figures personifying the Nile and Tiber, and many other pieces of classical sculpture, so that the court of the Belvedere came to be known as the "Antiquarium of Statues." Some of these works were on view in the gardens among the orange trees and laurels, others were kept behind wooden shutters in niches designed by Bramante; in one of these the *Venus Felix* may still be seen today.

Over the entrance to this garden with its priceless works of art stood the inscription: *procul esto profani*—"Keep aloof, ye that are uninitiated." In the Belvedere palace many of the artists who worked for Julius II and then for Leo X had lodgings or studios (Leonardo da Vinci, among others); and in the garden court there were always painters and sculptors at work, whether apprentices or masters, all with equal humility intently copying those fabulous marbles.

In 1566 Pius V (1566-1572), the pope of the Counter-Reformation, presented to the Roman People, that is to say to the Campidoglio, some of the most conspicuously profane of the statues in the Belvedere gardens, but the most famous pieces remained there, and are still there today. The Belvedere collection was not greatly enriched in the following century and preserved its singular character, that of a walled pleasure-garden or "academy," until the second half of the eighteenth century, when the writings of Lanzi and Winckelmann established art history and archaeology on a scientific basis, superseding the biographical methods modelled on Vasari's *Lives* and the "antiquarian" erudition of the Renaissance humanists and their followers. Herewith the Arcadian "gardens of statues" dear to the humanists began to give place to the first modern museums.

The second phase in the development of the Vatican Museums was initiated by Pope Clement XI (1700-1721), who drew up plans for bringing together the inscriptions —pagan inscriptions as well as those of the Catacombs—and housing them in suitable premises; he also made the first attempt to found a museum of Christian antiquities in the Apostolic Palaces. Though unfulfilled at Clement's death, these projects were carried out by his successors, in particular by Benedict XIV (1740-1758), the true founder of the Vatican Museums. He was responsible for the creation of the Galleria Lapidaria, the Gallery of Inscriptions, then housed in the corridor on the east side of the court of the Belvedere, where the Chiaramonti Museum now is; and for that of the Museo Sacro on the south side of the west section, where it remains today. Francesco Vettori, the munificent donor of a remarkable collection of ancient gems, was appointed curator of the new museum, instituted, according to the commemorative inscription, *ad augendum Urbis splendorem et asserendam Religionis veritatem*, and inaugurated in 1756.

The Museo Profano, planned by Benedict XIV, was actually founded by his immediate successor, Clement XIII (1758-1769); it too still occupies its original premises on the north side of the west corridor, next door to the Library. An inscription above the entrance records that these rooms were opened, in 1765, *curante Alex. Diac. Card. Albano, S.R.E. Bibliothecario*. This refers to Cardinal Alessandro Albani, nephew of Pope Clement XI and owner of a splendid collection of paintings and antique sculptures on view in his villa in the Via Salaria; he played a key part in the creation of the Museo Profano and gave the directorship to Winckelmann, who had already been appointed Prefect of Antiquities by Clement XIII. In his absence from Rome Winckelmann named Giovanni Battista Visconti as acting curator, and the latter succeeded him at his death in 1768. The first room of the Museo Profano preserves intact, both in the decoration and furnishings, its original aspect of a *cabinet de curiosités*, and is a typical example of an eighteenth century museum. The objects, chiefly ancient ivories from the Carpegna Collection, were displayed with more taste than method in elegantly carved cabinets lavishly adorned with gilt bronze fittings, built under Pius VI by Luigi Valadier with costly woods brought from Brazil; hence the four stars of the Southern Cross decorating the doors.

The Museo Sacro and the Museo Profano, which did not assume their final form until the pontificate of Pius VI (1775-1799), include the collection of Cardinal Gualtieri, of some two hundred Greek and Etruscan vases; Cardinal Albani's collection of coins and medals acquired by Clement XIII; the Carpegna Collection of gems, cameos, ivories and bronzes largely from the Catacombs, purchased by Benedict XIV; and the collection presented by Francesco Vettori, referred to above.

To the same period in the history of the Vatican Museums belongs the Pio-Clementino Museum, founded by Clement XIV (1769-1774), whose reign benefited the arts more than it did the Church. The new museum was intended to bring together the ancient statues and reliefs scattered in different parts of the Vatican; to house the marbles which, as a result of the laws enacted by Benedict XIV prohibiting the export of newly excavated antiquities, were accumulating in the Campidoglio and the Vatican; and, lastly, to provide suitable premises for the many pieces of sculpture acquired by the munificent, art-loving pope, among them the *Amazon,* the so-called *Pudicitia,* the *Centocelle Cupid* and the famous *Running Girl.*

The architect Michelangelo Simonetti joined the Museo Profano to the Belvedere of Innocent VIII by means of a monumental staircase (which still bears his name) and a succession of sumptuous rooms known as the Rotunda, the Hall of the Greek Cross, the Hall of the Muses (with ceiling frescoes by Tommaso Conca) and the Hall of Animals. Unfortunately, to make way for the latter, which adjoins the open gallery of the Belvedere, the small Chapel of St John, entirely decorated with frescoes by Mantegna, was ruthlessly destroyed; not a trace remains. These and further changes gravely impaired the original architecture of the Quattrocento summer palace, which was now embodied in the new museum. Into the projecting part on the east side was built the Cabinet of Masks, in itself an elegant example of eighteenth century decoration, adorned with mythological paintings by Domenico de Angelis. There now disappeared the already scanty remains of Pinturicchio's landscapes with urban views on the south side of the loggia, which was transformed into the Gallery of Statues; and the ceiling decorations were "restored" in the usual manner of that period, that is to say they were repainted. The two small rooms then added to the loggia by the pope are today occupied by the Gallery of Busts. The aspect of the Cortile, the garden court where statues were placed, was altogether changed; there Simonetti built a graceful portico round the central garden; under the portico, in the four corners of the court, now stand the *Laocoön,* the *Apollo Belvedere,* the *Hermes* of Praxiteles, and the *Perseus* of Canova, the last added by Pius VII. The Hall of the Biga, with the two *Discus Throwers,* is located in the upper storey of the entrance pavilion giving on the Stradone dei Musei. This well-proportioned edifice was erected by the Roman architect Giuseppe Camporesi in 1784; it clearly reflects the transition from the late Baroque to the neo-classical style.

Begun under Clement XIV, the grandiose complex connected with Bramante's Corridor by way of the Vestibule of the Torso was built, for the most part, under Pius VI (1775-1799), who filled it with some six hundred newly acquired works and opened the rooms to the public in 1787, thus setting an example later followed by many other rulers in Europe. This part of the papal collections is fittingly called the Pio-Clementino Museum, in honour of these two popes.

In 1797, ten years after the inauguration of the new rooms, the unfortunate Treaty of Tolentino, concluded between the Holy See and the conquering armies of Bonaparte, deprived the Papal States and the Vatican Museums and Library of their most precious art treasures and manuscripts. This sad interlude was brought to a close by the fall of Napoleon and the Congress of Vienna in 1815, which ordered the restitution of nearly all the works appropriated by the French, which for the most part had been placed in the Louvre. Thus began, in the pontificate of Pius VII (1800-1823) and under the superintendence of Canova, a third phase, the neo-classical phase, in the history of the Vatican Museums, memorable above all for the construction of the so-called Braccio Nuovo, the opening of the Pinacoteca and the Gallery of Tapestries, and the re-establishment of the cabinet of medals in the Library, only a small part of the original numismatic collection having been recovered.

The Pinacoteca was made up of pictures already owned by the Vatican and of some of the finest of the paintings recovered from France but not returned to their places of origin; for example, the *Coronation of the Virgin*, the *Foligno Madonna* and the *Transfiguration*, three of Raphael's masterpieces originally in the church of San Francesco at Perugia, the Convento delle Contesse at Foligno and San Pietro in Montorio at Rome, respectively; and other works like the *Deposition* of Caravaggio, formerly in a chapel of the Chiesa Nuova. No building was erected at that time to house the new collection of paintings, which were exhibited to the public in the rooms of the Borgia Apartment, where they could not be seen to advantage on account of the inadequate lighting and lack of space, and above all because the exuberant style of Pinturicchio's decorations was so much out of keeping with that of the later paintings exhibited there, in particular those of the seventeenth century. And in fact, for many years to come, down to the pontificate of Pius XI, the Pinacoteca had no permanent premises, being continually shifted from one part of the Vatican to another.

Pius VII (1800-1823), from the very beginning of his reign, encouraged fresh excavations and bought extensively on the art market in an attempt to make good the heavy losses sustained by the Vatican Museums as a result of the Treaty of Tolentino. In 1807 the smaller statues, busts and sarcophagi were removed to the north end of Bramante's Corridor, which has since been known as the Chiaramonti Museum (the family name of Pius VII), while the Gallery of Inscriptions, located here by Benedict XIV, was moved to the south end of the corridor, where it remains today.

With the return of the works of art appropriated by Napoleon and the ensuing reorganization of the Vatican collections, the problem arose of finding room for them and exhibiting them in a gallery answering to the modern idea of a museum, which was then taking form. This was the origin of the Braccio Nuovo, or New Wing, devoted to the larger and more famous works of sculpture. It extends across the court of the Belvedere from east to west, between the Library and the Pigna. The new building was designed by Raffaele Stern in the purest neo-classical style, with antique columns of precious marble, a barrel vault, dormer windows and niches in the walls for the statues. The lighting from above, as in an artist's studio, and the sobriety of the decoration (a single frieze in low relief with mythological scenes) prove that the architect's prime concern was to build a hall in which the works of art on display would show to best advantage; whereas the sculptures exhibited in the rooms built by

Simonetti seem to be placed there as ornaments. While the arrangement of the Pio-Clementino Museum is very much like that of a princely collection of the eighteenth century, the Braccio Nuovo, on the contrary, is already a museum in the modern sense of the term.

The famous Raphael tapestries of the Scuola Vecchia and the Scuola Nuova, carried off several times, were finally restored to the Vatican after 1815, in a precarious state of preservation. They were installed in a gallery and several chambers of the Apartment of Pius V, on the second floor at the west end of the Belvedere Corridor.

The papal collections took their present form under Gregory XVI (1831-1846) with the opening of three other museums: the Etruscan and Egyptian Museums and the Museo Profano in the Lateran Palace. The first, installed on the second floor of the building erected for Pius IV by Pirro Ligorio on either side of the Nicchione, was inaugurated in 1837. As a result of the edict of Cardinal Pacca, which reinforced the previous legislation of Benedict XIV regulating the disposal of excavated works of art and forbidding them to be exported, the new museum was enriched with an abundance of Etruscan, Italic and Greek works, brought to light for the most part in the lately discovered necropolis of Cerveteri (Regolini-Galassi Tomb).

The Egyptian Museum, housed on the first floor of the same building and opened to the public in 1839, grouped together not only many papyri and small objects acquired by Gregory XVI, but also Egyptian monuments from the Temple of Isis in the Campo Marzio, the Villa Adriana at Tivoli, the Borgia Collection at Velletri and other private collections (Gaddi, Palin, Guidi and Gavazzi).

In the Museo Profano in the Lateran Palace, inaugurated in 1844, were exhibited a great many Roman reliefs, statues, sarcophagi and mosaics for which there was no room in the Vatican, in addition to some outstanding paintings later removed to the Pinacoteca.

Later popes improved but did not substantially modify the form given to the Vatican Museums under Gregory XVI. In 1854, beside the Museo Profano in the Lateran Palace, Pius IX (1846-1878) established the Museum of Christian Art and appointed Father Giuseppe Marchi, S. J., as curator; he was assisted by the youthful Giovanni Battista de Rossi, who subsequently became the leading authority on early Christian art. The Gallery of the Candelabra was created by Leo XIII (1878-1903), who also restored the Borgia Apartment and opened it to the public. The Pinacoteca, enriched with Byzantine and Italo-Greek panels from the Vatican Library, was installed by Pius X (1903-1914) in new premises on the ground floor at the south end of the Belvedere Corridor; it was moved to its present and far more spacious building by Pius XI (1922-1939), who also founded the Ethnological Museum in the Lateran Palace.

Pius XII (1939-1958) arranged for contemporary art to be represented in the Pinacoteca by outstanding works, now on exhibit in two new rooms opened in 1960 under His Holiness Pope John XXIII.

•

The Vatican Museums are both custodians of works of art and works of art themselves. In the foregoing pages (as the reader will have noticed) no mention has been made of the Sistine Chapel, the Chapel of Nicholas V, the Stanze and Loggie of Raphael, the Borgia Apartment, all of which form part of the Vatican but have no place in the story of the Vatican Museums, with which alone this Introduction is concerned; they will be dealt with at length in the main text of the book. The same might be said, moreover, of the exhibition rooms, or of rooms built for that purpose, those for example of the Pio-Clementino Museum.

No little credit is due to the authorities in charge of the pontifical collections for having understood how much of their interest lies in the great diversity of the different galleries. Irregular in plan and composed of parts constructed at different times, they vividly reflect the changes of taste and aesthetic thought in the course of the centuries. Thanks to the care with which, wherever possible, their historical character and period setting have been preserved, the Vatican Museums illustrate the changing conceptions, from the Renaissance to our day, of what a museum should be.

But the great message which the Church of Rome addresses to the world through the medium of the Vatican Museums and the Vatican Library is the same as that embodied and illustrated in Raphael's frescoes, painted to the order of Julius II, in the Stanza della Segnatura: the ideal of Christian humanism, of the harmonious development of all the faculties of the human mind, on the natural and the spiritual plane, to the greater glory of God.

THE ARTS IN THE VATICAN

MAURIZIO CALVESI

THE EMPEROR AUGUSTUS. ROMAN SCULPTURE OF THE LATE FIRST CENTURY B.C. CHIARAMONTI MUSEUM, BRACCIO NUOVO.

I

THE FIRST BASILICA

According to an ancient tradition, the Basilica of St Peter's stands on the spot where the Apostle Peter was buried after suffering martyrdom. Excavations carried out during the pontificate of Pius XII have not only confirmed this tradition but shown that the Apostle's grave lies beneath the Altar of the Confession, under the great dome raised by Michelangelo. Deriving its distant origin from the martyrdom and death of the Chief Apostle, the Vatican Basilica can thus trace its history back to the earliest days of the Church and of Christianity itself.

Christianity found the requisite conditions for its growth and initial diffusion in the Roman Empire of the first century, which had subdued its neighbours, near and far, and united the ancient world under a single, universal authority. In forfeiting their freedom for the benefits of Roman civilization, the subject peoples gradually lost much of their individuality; and the gods they worshipped lost much of theirs, as reciprocal contacts and exchanges gradually modified them and drained them of their original meaning. "Since the territory of the Empire was called *orbis*," wrote Leopold von Ranke in his classic *History of the Popes*, "its inhabitants felt themselves to be a single, homogeneous people. Mankind was beginning to realize that all men share a common nature." Such was the world into which Christ brought tidings of the Kingdom of God, and from the dissolution of the old mythologies the new religion was born.

The statue of Augustus from Prima Porta opens this survey of the art treasures of the Vatican and St Peter's, which, in so far as possible, will be conducted on strictly historical lines, for the purpose of bringing a representative selection of works of art into relation with the history of the Church. The great statue of Augustus is illuminating in its own right, for what it stands for, over and above its aesthetic value. The sweeping gesture of the arm, almost like a secular benediction *urbi et orbi*, the broad, self-contained, soberly balanced rhythm of the body, the thoughtful composure of the handsome features, all go to express power and authority exercised with lordly

3

serenity and justice. This is the image of the emperor-god, commanding the reverence and veneration of his subjects, who in return enjoy protection and security. The canons of formal equilibrium and sculptural plenitude are those of classical art. But the sublimated force of classical Greek statuary, its contemplative longing for ideal beauty, its abstract and emotive cult of harmony, are absent. An ideal outlook has given place to a practical view of things. The formal means of classicism—i.e. its idealization of form—are enlisted in the service of government and statesmanship; they serve an active, not a contemplative purpose. Aesthetic harmony is no longer an *a priori* ideal, but the symbol, *a posteriori*, of political aspirations.

With its timely, solacing message, calling on men to minister to the superior aspirations of the soul, the Christian religion filled this immense spiritual vacuum. The Roman Empire, with its materialistic view of life and its vast physical expanse and uniformity, might be likened to the mould, the empty form, into which Christianity poured the life-giving plasma of the Faith.

The new religion came as a reawakened consciousness of higher things, directing the mind away from selfish motives and worldly ambitions towards the life to come, the Kingdom of God, where the righteous soul will find release from the tribulations of the flesh. In a sense Christianity was an ideological revolt—no other means of resistance being possible—of the humble against the strong. But it would never have achieved so much if, while soothing the painful consciousness of social inferiority that oppressed the humbler classes of society, it had not also appealed to the prevailing sense of bewilderment and futility, of moral frustration, with which Epicurean paganism had infected the upper classes of Roman society. Several centuries elapsed, however, before the different psychological and historical forces coming into play from various sources, and all working in the Church's favour, coalesced into a coherent attitude to life and gave rise to a new vision of the world, a new intellectual culture and a new artistic idiom. The cultural heritage of classical antiquity, particularly in its Hellenistic form, continued to bulk large. For Christian art began by taking over the styles and techniques of Hellenistic art and using them to express the ideals and symbols of the new religion.

St Peter came to Rome to spread the Word of God, and in Rome, in the reign of Nero (54-68), he was crucified (head downwards, at his own request, as recorded by the third century Alexandrian theologian Origen). The tradition of his journey to Rome and his martyrdom there is substantiated by historical evidence, some of it going back to the first century. As for the actual place where he was crucified, all the ancient sources are in agreement. Tacitus, in his *Annals*, tells us that during the reign of Nero, when the persecutions were at their height, the Christians were martyred in the Gardens of Nero—more exactly, in the Circus of Nero that stood in the Gardens. An ancient, anonymous account of the martyrdom of St Peter, written in Rome no earlier than the fourth century, states that the Apostle was crucified "near the Obelisk of Nero, towards the hill." St Jerome, writing in the fourth century, says that the crucifixion of Peter took place "on the Vatican." The *Liber Pontificalis*, which goes back to the sixth century, records that the Apostle was buried hard by the place of his martyrdom, "near the Palace (i.e. Circus) of Nero, on the Vatican."

The place of martyrdom, then, was the Vatican field, an area originally belonging to the Etruscans and included in the precincts of the city of Rome (though it remained outside the city walls) after the fall of Veii (396 B.C.). In the reign of Augustus (27 B.C.-A.D. 14), who divided Rome into fourteen regions, or wards, the Vatican was located in the fourteenth, which extended beyond the Tiber. This is the part of Rome occupied today by the Prati quarter and the Borghi, between the Tiber, Monte Mario, the Janiculum hill and the intervening heights, which in ancient times were called the "Vatican hills." This was originally an unhealthy, malarial area, subject to periodic floods; but in the first century A.D. it was partially reclaimed and gardens were laid out, known as the Gardens of Nero. There Caligula began the construction of a circus, finished by Nero, who was inordinately fond of public games and took part in them personally, driving his own chariot. Here were staged, for the amusement of the populace, the persecutions of Christians recorded by Tacitus, and it was here that St Peter was crucified. In the Circus of Nero stood an obelisk brought from Egypt—the same that stands today in the centre of St Peter's Square, where Pope Sixtus V had it erected in 1586 by Domenico Fontana.

In ancient times there were also tombs in the Vatican area. Recent excavations have brought to light, under St Peter's itself, a necropolis composed of rich sepulchral edifices, none of which, however, can be earlier than A.D. 130. But in the same cemetery are other tombs going back to the first century. There seems to have been a whole row of them which, following the line now marked by the Via della Conciliazione, ran across the present site of St Peter's Square and under St Peter's itself. It was in one of these tombs that the Apostle Peter was buried.

The *Liber Pontificalis* records that the Apostle was buried near the place of his martyrdom, and other accounts concur on this point. The archaeological evidence seems to leave no room for doubt. Excavations have unearthed a funerary shrine with niches, contrived in one of the walls of the second and third century necropolis mentioned above, datable to about A.D. 160 and showing traces of successive alterations (all however antedating the construction by Constantine of Old St Peter's). The shrine lies directly beneath the Altar of the Confession (in the present basilica), and its successive modifications show it to have been an object of special veneration until, after 315, Constantine decided to erect on the spot, first a grandiose *martyrium* in honour of the Apostle, then the original Basilica of St Peter's. For this, complex and extensive building operations were required in order to lay the foundations around and over the spot on which the Apostle's shrine stood. Soundings beneath the shrine itself

TOMB OF THE VALERII. SECOND CENTURY A.D. VATICAN NECROPOLIS.

Brought to light in recent excavations, the tomb of the Valerii is one of the richest and most impressive of the mausolea in the ancient necropolis located under St Peter's. The inscription over the entrance states that this was the tomb of C. Valerius Herma and his family. Further inscriptions discovered inside record the names of members of this and related families. The first dead to be buried here were pagans, but as Christianity grew and spread the tomb became in time a place of Christian burial.

The decoration of the tomb of the Julii in the same cemetery is, on the other hand, of distinctly Christian inspiration. As long ago as the sixteenth century, when St Peter's was being rebuilt, there were tentative explorations of the underground vaults beneath the church. Canon Tiberio Alfarano recorded in 1574 that, in the course of laying foundations for the columns in front of the papal altar, a tomb was discovered "all in antique mosaics with figures that appear to be horses." He was almost certainly referring to this very tomb. The chariot drawn by four horses was the traditional attribute of Apollo, here assimilated to the image of Christ interpreted as Helios or the sun god.

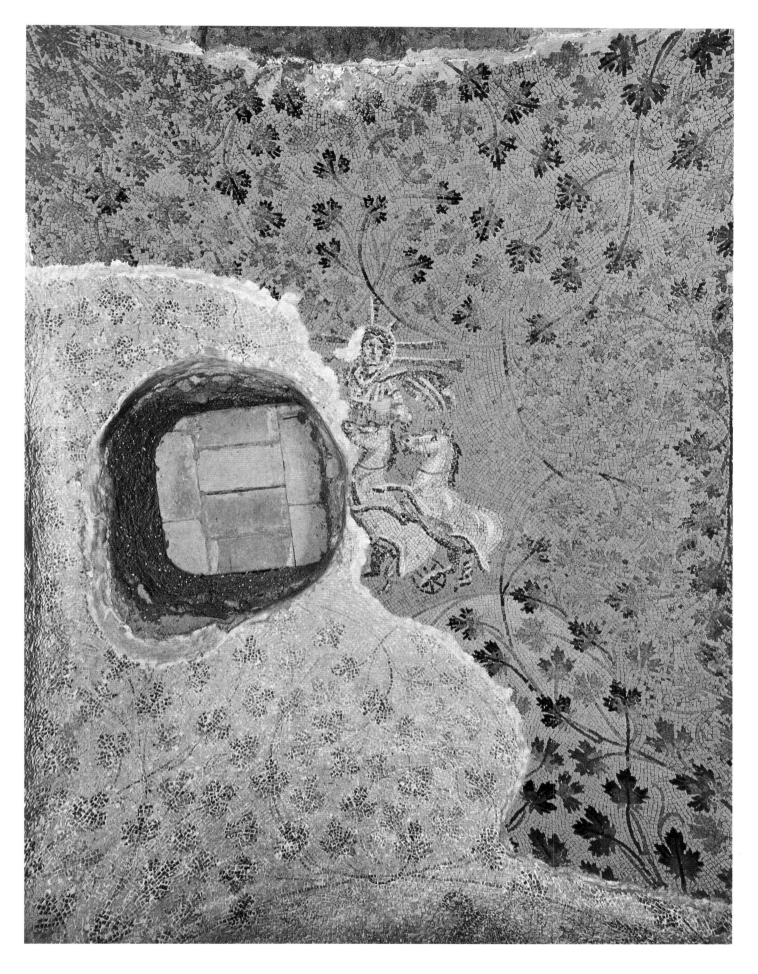

CEILING MOSAIC IN THE TOMB OF THE JULII: CHRIST AS THE SUN GOD. THIRD CENTURY. VATICAN NECROPOLIS.

7

have revealed traces of an ancient grave (which may well be the original grave of St Peter), while an ancient Greek inscription near the shrine, also datable to about A.D. 160, reads: "Herein is Peter." In the immediate vicinity of the shrine, moreover, are further traces of veneration (inscriptions, coins, etc.) going back at least as far as the second century A.D.

The extensive pre-Constantinian necropolis of the second and third centuries brought to light in the Vatican excavations, while consisting largely of pagan tombs, also presents certain Christian features in addition to the traces of Christian worship visible round the shrine of the Apostle. It is in fact—and this is quite unusual—a mixed cemetery. The nucleus is formed by a double row of brick burial chambers facing each other along a narrow corridor. The dead were either inhumed or cremated; hence the niches alongside both the sarcophagi and the tombs dug in the earth, containing urns in which the ashes were placed. Walls and vaults show traces of painted decorations (bowls of fruit, flowers, birds, small genii) intended to brighten the abode of the dead. One of the richest, most characteristic burial vaults is that of the Valerii (the name figures on a large stone embedded in the wall over the entrance), decorated with elegantly moulded bas-reliefs in stucco, in a lively and polished style, dating to the second half of the second century; some of them have crumbled away, but their outlines remain clearly discernible.

The combination of pagan cults and mythologies is typical of the cosmopolitan confusion of races and creeds in ancient Rome. Greco-Roman and exotic gods figure side by side in the cemetery: Minerva and Dionysus-Bacchus, Isis, Apollo-Harpocrates and Jupiter Dolichenus. But in the burial vault of the Valerii Christian elements also appear: several inscriptions and two sketchy paintings, now all but indistinguishable, of Christ and St Peter. These were added to the original tomb in the course of the third and fourth centuries, at a time, that is, when the new religion was rapidly increasing the number of its converts.

Even more typical, as illustrating the transition from the pagan cult to Christian worship, is the burial vault of the Julii. Originally a pagan *sacellum* (as shown by the remains of cinerary urns), it was converted into a Christian tomb in the first half of the third century. The interior is decorated with mosaics—a rare and costly technique which shows that the donors were well-to-do and could afford the best. The mosaic tesserae on the walls have nearly all fallen to the ground, but the outlines of the different scenes are still visible, representing the Good Shepherd, the Miraculous Draught of Fishes, and stories of the Prophet Jonah. The ceiling mosaic is better preserved and shows the figure of the Redeemer with the attributes of Apollo (quadriga and horses), surrounded by a verdant network of vine shoots. The figure, in which white predominates, is laid out longitudinally. Seen in the warm glow of the golden yellow ground, it is meant to convey a movement of ascension and suggest the consolations of the Resurrection. The dark outlines are thick and sketchy. In the vibrant juxta-position of the cubes, the mosaic imitates the "compendious" or "impressionistic" technique of Hellenistic painting. Prior to the discovery of this work, the earliest known example of a Christian mosaic was the decoration of the mausoleum of Santa Costanza in Rome, belonging to the fourth century. In the vault of Santa Costanza the mosaic cubes are disposed irregularly in order to create a pictorial effect whose unity and vividness are only apparent when seen from an appropriate distance. The ceiling of the tomb chamber of the Julii, on the other hand, is extremely low and the mosaic is seen from close at hand; for this reason the tesserae employed are much smaller, more thickly and evenly clustered, and undoubtedly less suggestive, though a certain concentration of light is achieved thanks to the fine-grained texture of the work.

This mosaic, however, is of particular interest for the way in which the image of Christ and the idea of the Resurrection are combined, both formally (thereby anti-cipating the handling of light and colour in Byzantine art) and iconographically, with

SARCOPHAGUS OF JUNIUS BASSUS. FOURTH CENTURY. VATICAN GROTTOES.

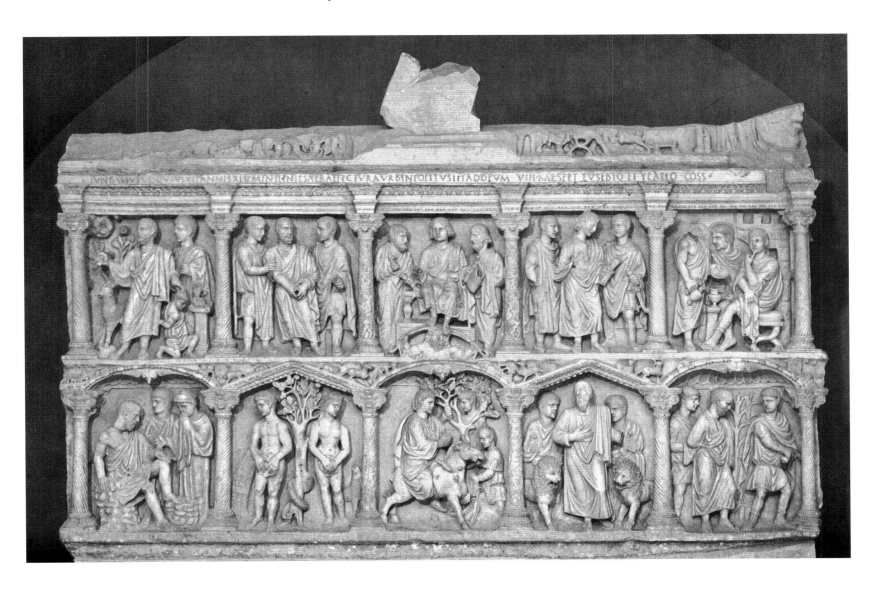

the theme of light as personified by Apollo (identified in late antiquity with the sun god Helios). From this it may be inferred that the pagan elements incorporated in the new Christian iconography were not always chance borrowings made for convenience' sake, but served rather as a means of reinterpreting, in a fresh light, symbols and motifs belonging to pagan creeds which, however different from Christianity, yet had something in common with it spiritually. From the Orphic and Dionysiac cults, for example, Early Christian art inherited many symbols (in the case of the mosaics in this tomb, the vine shoots, a Bacchic motif, and the image of the Good Shepherd, which derives from that of Orpheus); and these cults were a tissue of mystical injunctions and metaphysical tenets, some of which, in maturer form, and invested with a more vibrant spiritual message, found a place in the Christian vision.

The pictorial effects peculiar to Hellenistic art also reappear in Early Christian sculpture, together with robust, full-bodied forms in the purest Greco-Roman tradition. Preserved in the Grotte Vaticane is an outstanding example of an Early Christian sarcophagus, that of Junius Bassus, prefect of Rome, who died in 357. Here the two styles, Hellenistic and Greco-Roman, seem to meet. The figures stand out in full relief, compact and elegant, rendered with painstaking anatomical accuracy; but this harmony of form is coupled with an emphatic chiaroscuro effect. The elaborate, minutely detailed ornamentation of the architectural setting creates a subtly vibrant atmosphere round the figures. Each of the scenes—taken from the Old and the New Testament—stands within a framework of shadow which brings out to the full the shimmering luminosity of the salient surfaces. Here, in effect, each scene is enclosed in its own niche, in contradistinction to the continuous narrative style of Roman historical bas-reliefs; but the diversity of the architectonic elements relieves the static rectilinearity of the setting, creating subtle variations which effectively superinduce an undercurrent of graceful animation. This art is the expression of a refined, aristocratic civilization, untroubled by any searchings of the conscience. There is, however, an all-pervading mildness in the softly rounded volumes, a suffused serenity in the measured order of the composition, clearly reflecting the new evangelical ideals.

There was as yet, however, no essential difference of style or expression between Christian and pagan art. This is evidenced in the so-called Vergilius Vaticanus, a pagan manuscript dating to the early fifth century. The handling of forms, which dissolve into a narrative carelessly articulated but set to a definite rhythm, and still placed within a broad and sturdy spatial setting, is closely akin to what we find in contemporary manuscripts of Christian inspiration. The disintegration of this perspective setting, and its reduction to an art of patterned surfaces devoid of plastic form, can be seen taking place concurrently in the successive phases of Christian art (until they give rise to the abstractionism of the new Byzantine idiom) and in those of contemporary Imperial art, which in fact, particularly in its provincial manifestations, seems to anticipate and prepare this new orientation of taste.

SARCOPHAGUS OF JUNIUS BASSUS, DETAIL: CHRIST BETWEEN THE APOSTLES PETER AND PAUL. FOURTH CENTURY. VATICAN GROTTOES.

NONANNIDOMUIREDICLAINONMILLICARINAE

MINIATURE FROM THE VERGILIUS VATICANUS: LAOCOÖN. FIFTH CENTURY. VATICAN LIBRARY.

Illustrated in this miniature from the Vergilius Vaticanus is the story of Laocoön who, with his two sons, was attacked and killed by a serpent while sacrificing at the altar. According to the version given by Virgil (*Aeneid*, Book II), Laocoön, who had warned the Trojans against the wooden horse left by the Greeks, was punished by Athena who was bent on the destruction of Troy. According to an older version of the story (which is the one illustrated by the marble group of the second century B.C. preserved in the Vatican and reproduced on page 125), Laocoön was sacrificed by Apollo in order to save part of the Trojan population.

Of Old St Peter's, the original basilica built by the Emperor Constantine the Great (324-337) over the tomb of the Apostle, we can form a pretty good idea from old prints and written descriptions of it. Excavations have brought to light the massive substructure and the extensive underpinning required to compensate for the slope of the ground. In front of the basilica stood a vast square, often crowded with pilgrims, and dotted with oratories and chapels. Thirty-five steps led up to a great atrium from which five doorways gave access to the church. The spacious interior consisted of a nave and double aisles, a broad transept and a single apse decorated with a mosaic showing Constantine presenting the church to Christ and St Peter.

Ancient accounts of St Peter's all testify to the extraordinary wealth of its decorations and furnishings, continually increased and renewed by the lavish donations of the emperors and votive offerings brought by pilgrims from all over the known world. Rare marbles, precious metals and woodwork, enamels, stained glass, textiles, gold and jewellery were to be found in profusion in the fabulous Treasure of St Peter's. Unfortunately the pillage and rapine of successive barbarians, in their disastrous incursions into Italy, down to the terrible sack of Rome by foreign mercenaries in 1527, scattered these priceless collections to the winds again and again, though each time the remnants were salvaged and they were patiently built up anew. After the final looting of the Napoleonic armies, virtually nothing was left. The present Treasure of St Peter's, made up for the most part of nineteenth and twentieth century works, accordingly gives but a pale reflection of its ancient splendour.

Even so, it still contains a few relics of great price. The oldest of these, which has miraculously survived all depredations, is the Crux Vaticana, a reliquary cross of silver gilt, studded with precious stones, dating back to the second half of the sixth century. It was a gift, probably a votive offering, from Justin II, Emperor of the East (563-578), as recorded in the inscription running along the four arms of the cross. It is inset with emeralds, hyacinths, alabaster, agates, aquamarines and jasper, in alternately round and rectangular settings. Originally it was further surrounded with a row of sixteen large Oriental pearls. If we compare it with another fine cross in the Museo Sacro, made of gold enhanced with an exquisite combination of opaque and translucid enamels, the work of Roman goldsmiths of the early ninth century, we see that here the contour line is more vividly rendered; the fixity and abstraction of the Oriental schema, present in all its solemnity in the Crux Vaticana, is much less marked in the later work. This hieratic fixity brings out the intrinsic value and costliness of the object, which is like the outward token of a profound and worshipful reverence. History records that the Empress Sophia, Justin's wife, contributed her own jewels to enrich the gift intended to dazzle Roman eyes with a reflection of the splendour and the faith of the East.

Notwithstanding the vicissitudes and adversities that befell the papacy during the Middle Ages, it was then, unquestionably, that the prestige of the popes was at its highest, then that their political authority was effectively sustained by the intensity of the prevailing religious sentiment and by the spell which the figure of the Vicar of Christ cast even over non-Christian peoples. The accumulated wealth of the Treasure of St Peter's must have been a magnificent testimony to the universal homage paid to the Church of Rome.

In the broad central nave of Old St Peter's stood altars and oratories containing relics and images of particular veneration. One of the richest of these shrines was the Oratory of Pope John VII (705-707), decorated with mosaics which were nearly all destroyed

RELIQUARY OF THE TRUE CROSS, FROM THE SANCTA SANCTORUM OF THE LATERAN. NINTH CENTURY. MUSEO SACRO.

RELIQUARY CROSS OF THE EMPEROR JUSTIN II, CALLED "CRUX VATICANA." SIXTH CENTURY. TREASURE OF ST PETER'S.

when the old basilica was torn down in the sixteenth century. Only a few fragments survive: part of an Adoration of the Magi now in Santa Maria in Cosmedin and the figure of the pope himself, as a donor holding a model of his oratory, now in the Grotte Vaticane. John VII was a Greek and during his pontificate the influence of Byzantine art in Rome was at its height. The Arab invasion and conquest of the Near East in the

The demolition of the ancient basilica of St Peter's, built by Constantine, began in the pontificate of Julius II in the first decade of the sixteenth century. But the east end of the nave (shown in this fresco) was spared, together with the great atrium forming the entrance, until the reconstruction of the apse, transept and dome was complete. This part of the nave was finally demolished under Paul V, when the architect Carlo Maderna completed the new church and added the façade (1607-1614).

FRESCO SHOWING THE NAVE OF OLD ST PETER'S AS IT WAS IN THE SIXTEENTH CENTURY SHORTLY BEFORE ITS DEMOLITION. VATICAN LIBRARY.

POPE JOHN VII. MOSAIC FRAGMENT FROM HIS ORATORY IN OLD ST PETER'S. EIGHTH CENTURY. VATICAN GROTTOES.

17

MINIATURE FROM THE BIBLE OF LEO THE PATRICIAN: MOSES RECEIVING THE TABLES
OF THE LAW. TENTH CENTURY. VATICAN LIBRARY.

Byzantine book illumination in the tenth century was characterized by a revival of classical taste which is most
brilliantly exemplified in the great Psalter in the Bibliothèque Nationale, Paris (MS Grec 139). With it may
be associated two famous manuscripts in the Vatican Library: the Bible of Leo the Patrician (in which we
often find interpretations of the same models as those of the Paris Psalter) and the Joshua Roll. An unbroken
sequence of scenes in the latter manuscript illustrates the story of Joshua as told in the Old Testament, with
the appropriate texts written in Greek, in a fine hand, at the foot of the pictures. The depiction of Joshua's
exploits may have been intended as an indirect commemoration of the triumphs of Byzantine arms in Palestine
in the tenth century.

seventh and eighth centuries had driven into exile large numbers of Greeks and Levantines, a great many of whom ultimately settled in Rome and played a prominent part in the life of the city. Suffice it to say that in this period there were thirteen popes of Greek or Oriental origin.

Byzantine influence makes itself clearly felt in the mosaic of John VII which, in spite of the restorations it has undergone, still retains the spontaneity of a direct portrait. Flattened against the background, the figure is quite devoid of physical density. The abstract values of the surface preclude any indication of depth or perspective. The gold ground dispels any sense of actual space, as a delicate scale of tenuous colours vibrate and dissolve in its light. The outlines, whose function is that of delimiting and emphasizing the different zones of colour without expressing plastic values, are delineated almost timidly, the better to bring out the meek and submissive attitude of the pope. The ideal of otherworldly transcendence peculiar to Byzantine art is realized here with none of the pomp and splendour of the great Oriental and Ravennate prototypes, but rather in terms of a devotional humility which tempers refinement with sobriety.

Byzantine painting has one of its antecedents in the pictorial vibrancy of Hellenistic art, and it was through this channel that it was able to retrieve and embody certain features of the apparently opposing style of classicism. Evidence of this appears in two of the most precious illuminated manuscripts still preserved in the Vatican Library: the Bible of Leo the Patrician and the Joshua Roll, both of which are products of that revival of classical taste which took place in Byzantine book illumination in the tenth century. The miniatures in the Bible of Leo are executed in a manner deriving

MINIATURE FROM THE JOSHUA ROLL: JOSHUA AND THE ISRAELITES SLAYING THE FIVE KINGS OF THE AMORITES. TENTH CENTURY. VATICAN LIBRARY.

THE LAST JUDGEMENT, SIGNED BY "JOHANNES" AND "NICOLAUS." ELEVENTH CENTURY. PINACOTECA VATICANA.

from the "compendious" technique of the ancients, with rapid jottings and bright patches of colours; the compositions are built up in alternating zones of light and shade, and the narrative moves at a brisk and spirited pace. We find a much more subdued range of colours, more orderly and better balanced composition, in the Joshua Roll, whose story unfolds in an unbroken sequence of miniatures. The master of the Joshua Roll also works in a sketch-like style deriving from classical antiquity, but he develops his themes in a more refined and aristocratic setting. In his deft and incisive linearism he combines a Hellenistic directness with the subtle transcendentalism of Byzantine art. The sense of rhythm appropriate to the continuous sequence of the pictures, the sober compositional schemes with their suggestive pauses at stated intervals, the chaste refinement of the colour harmonies based on a few recurrent tones of reddish brown and blue, which even suffice to enliven several delightful landscape backgrounds—these are qualities indicative of a singularly gifted artist.

With the passing of this period of intense Byzantine influence, painting in Rome slowly awoke to a sense of its own resources. New stylistic features began emerging in the eleventh century, pointing the way to the new modes of expression of Romanesque art. The outstanding manifestation of this trend, in which for the first time we see a genuine Roman school of painting on the rise, is the fresco cycle in the church of San Clemente in Rome. To the Roman school of the same period belongs an unusual painting on canvas mounted on wood, of a peculiar shape (round, with a rectangular extension at the bottom forming a predella), representing the Last Judgement and first published in 1935 by Redig de Campos, shortly after it entered the Pinacoteca Vaticana. Probably painted about 1080, a dating also borne out by the written characters of the inscription, it comes in all likelihood from a chapel in the Benedictine convent of Santo Stefano "ad beatum Paulum"—the convent beside the basilica of San Paolo in Rome. It bears the signatures of "Johannes" and "Nicolaus," the same artists who signed the frescoes with Apocalypse scenes in the church of Sant'Elia at Nepi (Latium), some forty miles north-east of Rome. The Vatican panel is especially important from the iconographic point of view, for it is one of the earliest large-scale paintings of the Last Judgement not only in Italy but in the entire West. Its artistic interest and the novelty of its style lie in the wealth of motifs and episodes, in the colourful articulation of the narrative, in the subtle elasticity of the figures, their movements unimpeded now by the rigid patterning of Byzantine art.

This survey of the art forms that flourished in and about the Vatican in the Middle Ages—a survey necessarily brief and fragmentary, often illustrated by indirect examples owing to the loss or dispersion of the original works—would be incomplete without some mention of ivories and textiles. One of the most interesting extant examples of the former is the ivory diptych executed to the order of one Odelricus, abbot of the monastery of Rambona (founded at the end of the ninth century). There is some uncertainty about its dating, but it probably goes back to the tenth century.

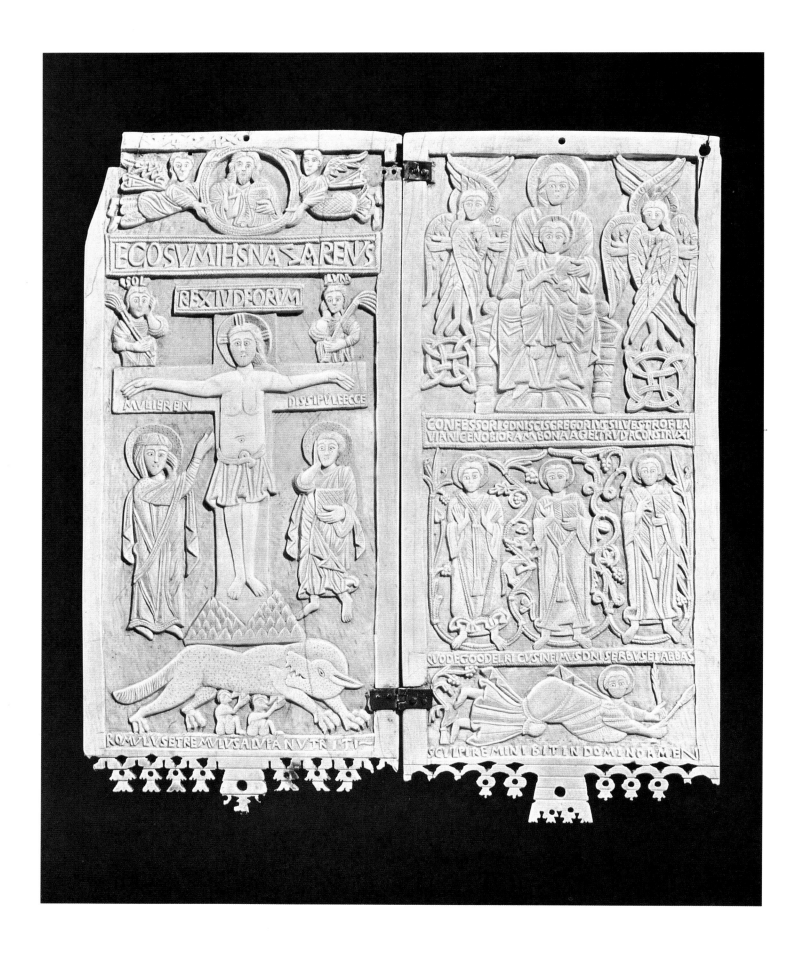

THE RAMBONA DIPTYCH. IVORY FROM THE MONASTERY OF RAMBONA. TENTH CENTURY (?). MUSEO SACRO.

BYZANTINE VESTMENT, THE SO-CALLED "DALMATIC OF CHARLEMAGNE." FOURTEENTH CENTURY. TREASURE OF ST PETER'S.

23

EMBROIDERED CLOTH. ORIENTAL ART OF THE EARLY MIDDLE AGES. MUSEO SACRO.

The relief is still low and flat, and the figures are shown frontally, but the formal refinements of Byzantine art have been forgotten. It has, on the contrary, a pointedness, a compelling immediacy of notation very different from the intellectual subtleties of the Byzantines. The symmetrical composition of each panel by no means rules out a certain vivacity, and indeed some very lively touches, in the presentation of the figures, calculated not so much to focus and rivet the spectator's attention as to awaken a direct interest in the narrative, and even an amused curiosity. The influence of barbarian reliefs and expressionistic modes borrowed from Northern miniatures is responsible for this divergence from the Byzantine norm, this reorientation of style, which prepared the way for the rise of Romanesque art.

Of outstanding interest among the textiles preserved in the Vatican are a rare and priceless example whose design is probably of Persian origin (all the textiles of the early Middle Ages now extant in Italy appear to be imported Oriental works) and the famous dalmatic which, according to tradition, was worn by Charlemagne during the coronation ceremony which took place in St Peter's on Christmas Day in the year 800, when he was crowned by the pope Emperor of the West. Actually, however, the style of the design argues strongly in favour of a dating subsequent to the ninth century; in fact, as Pietro Toesca has shown, it is almost certainly the work of Byzantine artists of the fourteenth century. Byzantine art seems to be rising here to the climax of that refined, almost ethereal tension that preceded its decline and dissolution. Woven in sky-blue silk darkened by age, the dalmatic is adorned with gold and silver embroidery; on one side is the Transfiguration, on the other the Last Judgement. It is a work of the highest quality and taste, combining solemnity of presentment with lightness and buoyancy of design. The figures, moving to an agreeable rhythm of supple, unbroken lines, are surrounded by a pattern of plant motifs and abstract symbols whose fanciful variety and finesse are worthy of a Far Eastern master.

This beautiful vestment conveys an idea of the gorgeous pageantry of the ceremonies performed in Old St Peter's in the Middle Ages when, as Jacob Burckhardt has written, "not the church but the officiant himself figured as a symbol and a programme, and was therefore enveloped in the costliest garments, which concealed his entire person from view."

2

THE LATE MIDDLE AGES

The donations of Pepin and the alliance with Charlemagne had enabled the papacy to regain the universal prestige that the break-up of the Roman Empire and schisms within the Church itself had seriously undermined. To all intents and purposes, it was the Carolingian dynasty that revived and endorsed the pope's prestige, which it needed as a kind of superior sanction. It only did so, of course, on condition that the papal power should remain subordinate to that of the emperor.

This state of affairs was radically changed by Gregory VII (1073-1085). Finding the German emperors embroiled in internal disorders and harried by rebellious princes, Gregory took vigorous steps to free the Church from imperial influence, and from secular interference generally. After a long struggle its independence was effectively established. Never had the Church wielded greater or more widespread power than in the thirteenth century. The splitting up of the empire into separate nations lent a glamour and appeal to the broad-based unity of the papacy.

But slowly that unity was undermined. Even by the end of the thirteenth century the formation of the European states was fostering a spirit of independence among the various nationalities. Men no longer felt the need of that spiritual community which in its day had bound Germans and Romans together in a common cause and laid the basis for the whole evolutionary process of Western civilization. One after another, the European states rose up against the authority of the Church, whose shaping influence on the lives of men and the policies of nations, for a time absolute, steadily declined.

It was at this crucial moment (in 1294) that Boniface VIII was elected pope, following the abdication of the ascetic hermit-saint Celestine V. "He shall come in like a fox, reign like a lion, and die like a dog": such is said to be the prophecy pronounced by Celestine V upon the advent of his successor; and it was fulfilled to the letter, in the most dramatic circumstances. After a fierce struggle, first against opposing factions in Rome, then against the king of France, the luckless Boniface succumbed to main force; thrown into prison, beaten and starved, he died indeed "like a dog" (1303).

Fond of pomp and pageantry, Boniface saw in art an instrument of authority, a means of glorifying the Church and the person of the pope, and he patronized the best artists of his time. Foremost among the sculptors then working in Rome, actually few in number and for the most part of small account, was Arnolfo di Cambio, an independent-minded artist schooled in the circle of Nicola Pisano. From him, among other works, Boniface commissioned a small chapel in St Peter's, which he intended as his own last resting place and hoped to see completed before he died. This chapel was demolished in the early seventeenth century when the last surviving portions of Old St Peter's were cleared away. All that now remains are the sarcophagus, which was removed to the Grotte Vaticane, and a few other fragments, among them a bust of Boniface VIII. A mediocre print in Ciampini's *De sacris aedificis* shows us what the chapel looked like. Over the altar stood a large pointed canopy resting on four columns, designed in a Gothic style of classical proportions, like the ciboria already executed in Rome by Arnolfo for the churches of San Paolo and Santa Cecilia. Above, fixed to the back wall of the chapel, was the sarcophagus with a recumbent statue of the pope, sur-mounted by a mosaic representing Boniface worshipping the Virgin.

An abundant production of works of art must have accompanied the proclamation in 1300 of the first Holy Year, which marked the highest point in the fortunes of the papal see under Boniface VIII. From all corners of Europe the faithful flocked to Rome in quest of the indulgences granted to pilgrims who, in the course of Holy Year, paid a visit to the basilicas of the Holy Apostles Peter and Paul. The churches remained open round the clock, thronged with people day and night. Some of the greatest men of the age—Dante, Giovanni Villani, Cimabue, Oderisi da Gubbio, Giotto—came to Rome in 1300 and mingled with the crowd. For the occasion Giotto painted a fresco in St John Lateran representing Boniface in the act of proclaiming the Jubilee.

It may have been in anticipation of the Jubilee that the pope commissioned Arnolfo to design the bronze statue of St Peter still standing in the main nave of the basilica, where it has been an object of veneration for centuries. This statue, whose existence was first recorded by Maffeo Vegio about the middle of the fifteenth century, was long an enigma to art historians. In the sixteenth century it was believed to be a remodelled piece of classical sculpture, originally representing Jupiter. Wickhoff, writing at the end of the nineteenth century, proved the groundlessness of this tradition, pointing out, for one thing, that the keys, the Apostle's iconographic attribute, were not a later addition but had been cast with the rest of the statue. Thereafter scholars were split into two camps. Most of them held it to be a Late Roman work datable to between the fourth and the sixth century. Others, including Wickhoff and Adolfo Venturi, ascribed it to the thirteenth century, assigning it to the entourage of Arnolfo di Cambio or to Arnolfo himself. Although the first hypothesis still finds a few die-hard supporters, the most recent conclusions of art scholarship all tend to confirm the attribution to the Tuscan sculptor. That the statue was actually made in the Gothic period is borne out by a technological examination of the bronze and by the method of casting (the uneven thickness of the metal shows that the statue was modelled directly in the wax, as was also to be the case with the statues of Ghiberti, Verrocchio and Cellini). And besides this the style tells heavily in favour of Arnolfo.

The pontificate of Boniface VIII marks a crisis in the history of the Church, whose hegemony was being challenged by the rise of independent states throughout Europe. Similarly the work of Arnolfo di Cambio marks a turning point in art history, led up to by Romanesque and made inevitable by Giotto: Arnolfo's art signalizes the break with medieval mysticism and Byzantine abstractionism and a decisive step towards man's realization of his unique individuality, his commanding position in the scheme of things, his passionate yearnings and the urgency of his feelings. Here were new forces at work: already stirring in Gothic art, they erupted in the Renaissance. The universality of the Byzantine idiom was challenged at last, and not only the writers but also the artists of each country began speaking a language of their own. The parallel so often—too often—drawn between Dante and Giotto also holds good for Arnolfo, provided it is not carried too far, for the aristocratic complexity of Dante's mind and art has no equivalent in the more direct, instinctive and, if not democratic, anyhow less intellectual conceptions of Arnolfo (and, for that matter, of Giotto himself). Certain it is, however, that clean-cut outlines and firmly moulded forms are common in this age to all the outstanding works of Italian art and literature. Through Arnolfo these national characteristics were fused to the archaic compactness of Etruscan statuary, and through Giotto to the spatiality and plasticism of the classical tradition.

The abstractions and mysticism of Byzantine art, and indeed the whole medieval way of seeing that lay immediately behind Arnolfo, no doubt conditioned this joint reversion to classicism and archaism, accounting for the solemn fixity of gaze that still gives these images the look of idols. This is particularly true of the statue of St Peter. It is no longer the bemused and vacuous fixity of the medieval icon, but has a milder quality that merges and makes one with the inner tension of the image, which seems to be in the act of curbing or repressing an unruly surge of feelings, a restless energy that ripples over its adamantine surface.

From 1736 on it became the custom to dress the bronze statue of St Peter in pontifical vestments; those used ▷ today date to the seventeenth and eighteenth centuries. Judging by its unusual dimensions, the magnificent triple tiara, made of gilded metal and silver, was probably executed expressly for this statue. The dressing of the statue takes place on June 29, the feast day of St Peter and St Paul, and on particularly solemn occasions, when the pope is present in the Vatican Basilica.

ARNOLFO DI CAMBIO (1232?-1302): STATUE OF ST PETER. BRONZE. NAVE OF ST PETER'S.

ARNOLFO DI CAMBIO'S STATUE OF ST PETER WITH THE PONTIFICAL VESTMENTS.

No sculptor could have conjured up the figure and features of the redoubtable Boniface more tellingly than Arnolfo has done in the recumbent effigy on the sarcophagus: a man stern and resolute of purpose, standing on his dignity like an ancient potentate, but swept up in the vortex of power politics from which, for one of his stubborn and passionate convictions, there was no release but death. The rigid body, squared up by a play of lines which has all the spareness, purity and elegance of a geometrical theorem, cleaves to the rectangular slab of the sarcophagus; but the sustained energy of the folds that furrow the robe and pattern the funerary drapery communicates a flickering tension to the whole, almost as if the life blood were coursing through the veins of the marble.

Again, no sculptor but Arnolfo could have conveyed so well, in the bronze statue of St Peter, the ideal of the *ecclesia imperialis* dear to Boniface, the ideal of a Church inheriting to the full the power and universality of the Rome of the Caesars and, on the strength of that unique and glorious heritage, dwarfing the pretensions of its enemies and rivals. Artistically, Arnolfo's embodiment of that ideal is not above criticism; in some respects it does not appear to be fully realized. But if the *facture* of this statue is less strikingly personal than that of Arnolfo's other works, the reason well may be that he was working from a model—a model readily identifiable in the earliest extant marble statue of St Peter, still preserved today in the Grotte Vaticane, which derives directly or indirectly from a classical prototype. Of that classicism Arnolfo retained—perhaps at the pope's instigation—not only the spirit but also the letter. The fact remains that, with its strong power of suggestion, the work fulfils the aim it was meant to fulfil. Through the centuries it has cast, and casts today, an extraordinary spell over the faithful: a figure at once forbidding and comforting, at once pastor and taskmaster; a bronze idol firmly poised on one leg, but seeming with the other about to rise graciously to its feet; obliging and even urbane in the movement of the legs and lower body, distant and inaccessible in the upward sweep of bust, neck and head, which form a self-containing space around them, like that of a niche. The right hand, upraised in blessing and solemnly punctuating its movements, marks the limit of that inviolable space, and all but transgresses it, while the other holds the keys tightly, the arm ingeniously supported by a kind of sling attached to the shoulder.

The fate of Boniface VIII was but one token of the growing power of the French king, Philip the Fair. The papacy had thrown off the yoke of the German emperors and asserted its independence only to be drawn now into the orbit of resurgent France. This situation was materially sanctioned when Clement V, a French pope who owed his elevation to Philip, removed the Holy See to Avignon in 1309. Clement was followed by six successive popes, all of them Frenchmen, who had their seat in Avignon, until the last of the six, Gregory XI, finally restored the papacy to Rome in 1377.

During the "Babylonian captivity" of the popes in Avignon, Rome sank to the level of a penurious and disorderly provincial backwater, and artistic production declined. In the early decades of the papal exile, however, St Peter's and the art treasures it housed were in good hands: those of Cardinal Jacopo Stefaneschi, a man of culture and learning, a doctor of canon law of the University of Paris, where he had also taught with signal success. He now turned to Giotto for a series of works designed to embellish the basilica, among them the great mosaic known as the "Navicella" and the so-called Stefaneschi Altarpiece in the Pinacoteca Vaticana. Documentary evidence proves these two works to have been commissioned from Giotto by Stefaneschi personally, but the exact dates are unrecorded.

ARNOLFO DI CAMBIO (1232?-1302): SARCOPHAGUS OF POPE BONIFACE VIII. VATICAN GROTTOES.

GIOTTO (1266?-1337): THE "NAVICELLA" MOSAIC, AS RESTORED IN THE SEVENTEENTH CENTURY. PORTICO OF ST PETER'S.

The "Navicella" mosaic, a work of monumental proportions (measuring approximately 31 by 44 feet), was originally located over the entrance of the great atrium of the Constantinian basilica, as shown in Paeseler's reconstruction. The mosaic stood facing the façade of the church, and the faithful, having entered the atrium, had to turn round to admire it. According to the account given by Francesco Maria Torriggio (in *Le Sacre Grotte Vaticane*, Viterbo 1618), "When pilgrims reached the doors of St Peter's, before entering the church they turned to the east, as if worshipping the sun; having noticed which, Cardinal Jacopo Stefaneschi, canon of St Peter's, resolved to put an end to this practice. And so to make them address their prayers to a sacred image, he had a very famous master of those days, called Giotto the Florentine, make a Boat in mosaic, which represents the Apostles sailing the sea, and beholding Christ walking on the waters, St Peter leaped from the boat and went to meet Him, as told by St John in the Gospel." The two medallions with angels (of which something has been said in the text) may have been located in the decorative border surrounding the main scene, or else on either side of the inscription that once figured beneath it. It has been suggested by Eugenio Battisti that the two angels may not have belonged to the "Navicella" at all, but formed part of the decoration on the inner walls of the church itself.

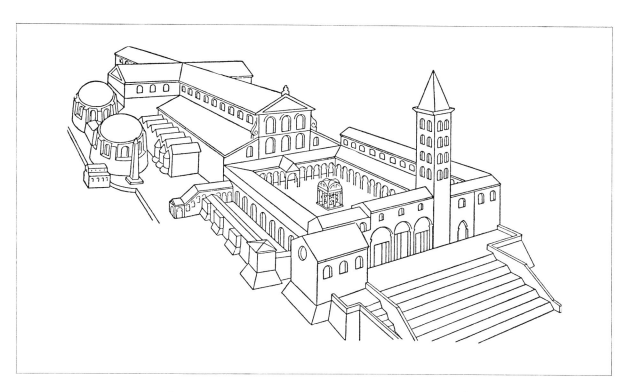

OLD ST PETER'S IN THE MIDDLE AGES. RECONSTRUCTION BY SCHÜLLER-PIROLI.

LOCATION OF GIOTTO'S "NAVICELLA" MOSAIC IN THE ATRIUM OF OLD ST PETER'S.
FROM THE DRAWING BY W. PAESELER.

Two seventeenth century chroniclers have handed down two different dates for the Navicella mosaic (1298 and 1320), but Lionello Venturi has shown that neither has any real foundation in fact. Giotto, as already mentioned, went to Rome for the Jubilee celebrations of 1300 and painted some frescoes in St John Lateran for Boniface VIII; many scholars accordingly assume that the Navicella was executed at the same time. But stylistic evidence, meagre though it is (for the mosaic was entirely restored in the seventeenth century), has oriented the most recent trend of Giotto studies towards a dating of about 1310, or shortly afterwards, a view borne out by a document of 1313 referring to a recent visit of Giotto to Rome.

All that now remains of the great mosaic, after the seventeenth century restoration, is the iconography and the general design; fortunately this can be supplemented by many copies of the lost original and by works deriving from it. The mosaic represents the ship (i.e. the "Navicella") of the Apostles caught in a storm on the Sea of Galilee (Matthew xiv), with St Peter walking on the waters towards Christ; but details of expression and the deeper significance of the scene now elude us. Probably the iconography was stipulated in detail by Cardinal Stefaneschi himself; and if, as appears almost certain, the work was commissioned, not at the time of the Jubilee rejoicings, but after the removal of the papacy to Avignon, then the scene may have been meant to allude to the stormy times through which the Roman Curia was passing, deserted by the popes and a prey to contending factions.

If one thing comes through clearly, it is the grandeur of the composition. The archaic frontality of the figure of Christ no longer has the abstract, undefined spatiality of its Byzantine prototypes, but with its full-bodied volumes serves as the stable point of departure from which the whole composition is built up and deployed. The surface of the water forms an orthogonal plane with respect to that of the sky and thus emphasizes, by a sharp perspective projection, the massive actuality of the figures occupying that plane. This powerful, compendious spatiality, conspicuously absent in the Assisi frescoes, is, rather, one of the achievements of Giotto's Paduan period (Scrovegni Chapel) and grows more marked in the works immediately following thereafter. Hence the advisability of a later dating for the Navicella.

When the mosaic was recast in 1610, Bishop Simoncelli of Boville Ernica (near Frosinone) removed to the church of his native town (where it still is) a mosaic medallion with a half-length angel accompanied by an inscription proving it to come from St Peter's and, more specifically, from the Navicella mosaic. This fragment is one of a pair; the other, now in the Grotte Vaticane, is mentioned by an early source as a work of Giotto's. So it too must have formed part of the Navicella, this medallion and the one at Boville Ernica thus representing the sole surviving fragments of the original work. Presumably these two half-length angels stood in the decorative border surrounding the main scene or on either side of the inscription that figured beneath it.

GIOTTO (1266?-1337): HALF-LENGTH ANGEL. MOSAIC MEDALLION FROM OLD ST PETER'S. VATICAN GROTTOES.

From Cardinal Jacopo Stefaneschi, nephew of Pope Boniface VIII, Giotto received several important commissions, notably the "Navicella" mosaic and the great altarpiece illustrated here, originally painted for the high altar of St Peter's. The central panel represents Christ Enthroned, surrounded by a double choir of angels; at the foot of the throne kneels the worshipping figure of the donor, Cardinal Stefaneschi—one of the earliest naturalistic portraits in Renaissance painting. The two side panels represent the Crucifixion of St Peter and the Decapitation of St Paul. At the base of the altarpiece are the predella scenes: in the centre, the Virgin and Child enthroned, attended by two angels and two saints; on either side stand five full-length figures of Apostles.

GIOTTO (1266?-1337) AND ASSISTANTS:
THE STEFANESCHI ALTARPIECE.
PINACOTECA VATICANA.

Seen against a vibrant blue ground, the angel stands out forcibly but serenely, with mild but firmly delineated features. It is like a voice from the past which, almost as if the solemn and splendid accents of Byzantine mysticism had never been, re-echoes the soft and gracious tones of certain Early Christian paintings, as do also some of the Ravenna mosaics. But instead of the indefinable serenity, staid and impersonal, of a transcendental vision, Giotto strikes a human, an individual note; instead of the formal apparitions of an earlier time, he gives us a living being. He does not speak to us in the name of fixed and unalterable metaphysical dogmas unquestioningly accepted, but in the name of hopes and expectations born of his knowledge of men and things, his insight into the springs of human feelings and actions, in a word his experience of daily life and earthbound realities. This mild-visaged angel is but one note in an infinitely varied scale, but one facet of the prism. At other times his painting rises or subsides to another pitch, tremulous or jubilant, sorrowful or dramatic, as the case may be; the full range may well have been spanned in the Navicella scene alone. What unifies his vision, over and above the play of emotions, is the purposefulness of every action represented, the spacious stage on which his figures move, and the echo of eternity with which their voices ring.

Seen in historical perspective from the viewpoint of today, that is from the existentialist viewpoint of the moderns, Renaissance man seems disturbingly like ourselves, already self-centred and guided by self-interest, engrossed in the problem of his own freedom of action. Man as pictured by Giotto is a fresh, unblighted creation, even though his image is reflected in the still unshattered mirror of medieval faith and the fullness of his physical reality is projected on to this motionless screen.

Giotto's early work, as exemplified by the Assisi frescoes, combined a full-bodied treatment of volumes with an unusual tautness of outline, the figures being grouped in a spatial setting essential to the narrative; he had points of contact with Arnolfo di Cambio, of whose outstanding abilities Giotto was well aware. In the work of his maturity, as his conception of space became more aulic, and his sense of volumes and masses grew stronger, Giotto's forms also became more receptive to the blandishments of colour and gradations of light. The two half-length angels in medallions from the Navicella mosaic are indicative of this shift of interest. Mosaic art in Rome had been treated with monumental breadth of design and an unfailing sense of colour values by Pietro Cavallini, one of the pioneers of Italian painting at the close of the thirteenth century. In acceding to this technique Giotto intuitively grasped its light and colour possibilities. Cavallini's mellow classicism undoubtedly appealed to him and stimulated him, but to the softened outlines of Cavallini's monumental figures, still imbued as they are with Byzantine hieraticism, Giotto consistently opposed a well-defined spatial setting. With Giotto, art drew deeper breaths and moved its limbs more freely, thanks to a breadth of space created by colour values which, at the same time, ensure an unprecedented clarity of definition.

As it matured, his art thus moved in the direction of a higher classicism. Emotional impulses, recorded and crystallized within an internal time continuum, go to form a compelling vision which, without losing contact with it, embraces reality from a height never before attained. The altarpiece commissioned by Cardinal Stefaneschi belongs to this mature phase of his art. We have no way of knowing the exact date of execution, but judging by the style it seems safe to say that it was painted after 1330. Though the quality of the design and workmanship remains high throughout, it is not a wholly autograph painting. Many parts of it reveal the hands of pupils—very fine pupils close in style to Giotto himself, but possessed of distinct personalities of their own, who must have been employed, and busily employed, in his studio in the closing years of the master's life when he was overburdened with commissions.

In the austere and imposing interior of the old basilica of St Peter's, this great altarpiece must have found an ideal setting. Giotto himself was undoubtedly responsible for the architectonic design of the whole, so grandly and elastically conceived, with the regular patterning of the partitions which mark off the limpid depths of the three main scenes and channel their rhythms into the apex of each panel. The central panel can only be by Giotto. "This is made quite clear," as Cesare Gnudi writes, "by the brilliant conception of the throne, whose architecture soars up towards the outer contour of the triple apex, in such a way that the latter forms a foreground with respect to the background formed by the gold surface of the panel itself; between these two planes the sides of the throne stand in perspective in the intervening space." The side panels too, with the *Crucifixion of St Peter* and the *Decapitation of St Paul*, though plainly by other hands, are such fresh and intense creations, and merge so smoothly into the general scheme of the altarpiece as a whole, that they must have been based on a preliminary design by Giotto himself. The two perspective vistas, with landscapes, are admirably balanced in relation to the internal perspective of the central scene, which forms the vital pivot on which this majestic vision turns. The words of Erwin Panofsky in his study of perspective apply particularly well to a painting like this. "The work of Giotto and Duccio marks the first step beyond the medieval principle of representation. For the representation of an internal space closed off and conceived as a hollow body involves more than a concrete consolidation; it amounts to a revolution in the formal evaluation of the picture surface. The latter is no longer the wall or panel on which the forms of particular things and figures are disposed, but is once again a transparent plane through which we fancy ourselves to be looking into an open space, although it is still bounded on all sides."

Giotto's influence was decisive in giving a new impulse and direction to Trecento Italian painting and his innovations had immediate repercussions on one of the most tradition-bound of all art forms: miniature painting. Two illuminated manuscripts of the early fourteenth century, preserved in the Vatican Library, illustrate the change that had come about. A codex of church laws, signed by Jacopino da Reggio, shows

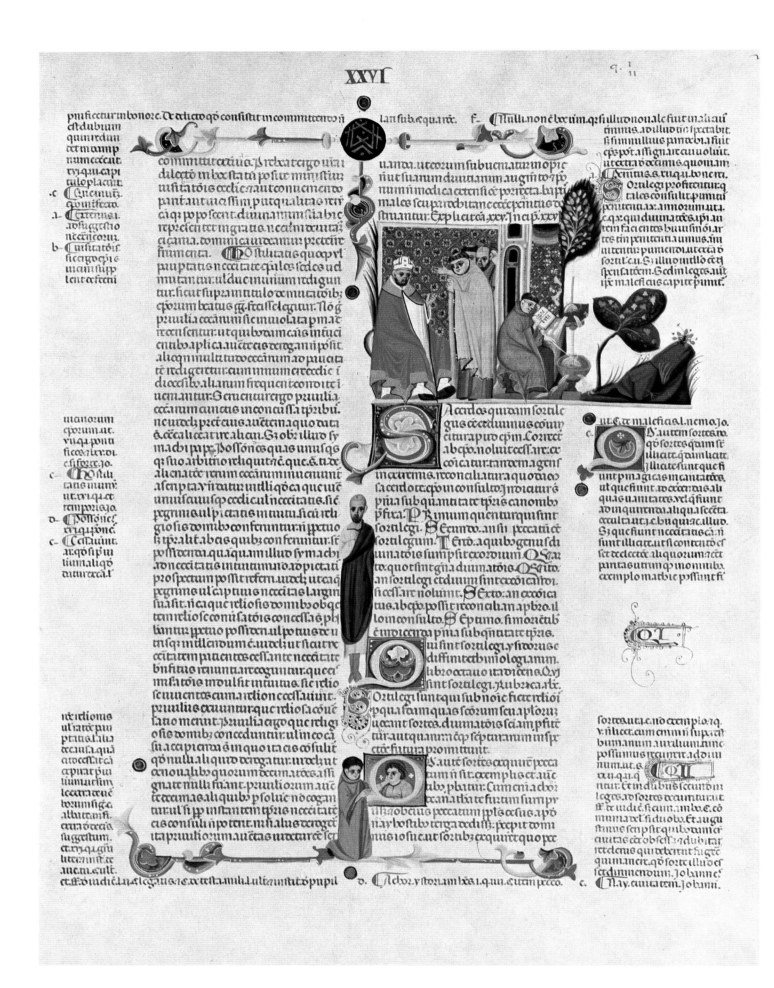

PAGE OF A CODEX OF CHURCH LAWS. MINIATURE PAINTING BY JACOPINO DA REGGIO. FOURTEENTH CENTURY. VATICAN LIBRARY.

42

all the refinements of a subtle, painstaking style of illumination in the traditional manner. The handwritten pages, neatly divided into two columns, are bordered by elegant, elongated figures; Byzantine influence is still paramount in the rigid frontality of the compositions, and in their minutely detailed, sophisticated handling. How different is the Apocalypse scene in another codex, also by an Emilian artist, Neri da Rimini (active between 1300 and 1322). His broad, synthetic brushwork and easy narrative style, which never lingers over small points of detail, already reflects Giotto's ascendancy and the new style on the rise, whose effects are particularly noticeable in the contemporary school of Rimini.

The great age of manuscript illumination had ended, and the very existence of this "minor" branch of painting was soon to be endangered. As the Renaissance grew and spread and changed men's outlook, the personality of the artist came to be recognized and indeed glorified as a thing apart from that of the craftsman—a distinction

APOCALYPSE SCENE. MINIATURE PAINTING BY NERI DA RIMINI. FOURTEENTH CENTURY. VATICAN LIBRARY.

RELIQUARY OF SAN BIAGIO (ST BLAISE), DATED 1402. NEAPOLITAN WORK. TREASURE OF ST PETER'S.

GOLD CHALICE, ABOUT 1340. FROM THE ABBEY OF SAN MARTINO AL CIMINO NEAR VITERBO. TREASURE OF ST PETER'S.

inconceivable in the Middle Ages—and the gulf between the major and the minor arts accordingly widened. Throughout the fourteenth century, however, the vitality of the latter remained unimpaired, and anonymous "craftsmen" continued to produce a wide variety of works of exquisite artistry.

The production of fine goldwork was particularly abundant and the basilica of St Peter's must have numbered some extraordinary pieces in the incomparable treasure of such objects which it once possessed—now unfortunately dispersed. Outstanding among the surviving works is a gold chalice, chased and enamelled, datable to about 1340. It is probably a work of the Abruzzi school, as may be inferred from its robust, almost architectonic lines, with no ornamental flourishes. It came originally from the abbey of San Martino al Cimino, near Viterbo, and only entered the treasure of St Peter's in 1601.

Another notable work, in the possession of the church of St Peter's since the fifteenth century, is a reliquary in gilded silver inset with enamels and glass pastes, containing a relic of St Blaise. Dating to 1402, it is designed in a light and agreeable style which reduces the soaring verticalism of Gothic to an architecture of superimposed planes, with a rhythmic alternation of full and empty spaces; with its mental calibration, it is typical of the craftsman's approach. Both the name of the donor (Henricus de Minutolis Cardinalis Napolitanus) and its stylistic characteristics show it to be a Neapolitan work.

3

THE PAPAL RESIDENCE

When Pope Martin V entered Rome in September 1420, on his way back from the Council of Constance which had put an end to the Great Schism, he was given an enthusiastic welcome. For the first time in one hundred and thirty-five years, a native Roman had been raised to the Holy See. The city itself had passed through a disastrous period of lawlessness and decay: buildings were dilapidated, the streets deserted and squalid. Rome scarcely resembled a city any longer: *"nulla urbis facies,"* wrote Platina.

Martin V took energetic steps to restore order and reassert the papal authority over the communal law. He drew up an extensive programme of reconstruction, restoring many churches and calling in artists like Gentile da Fabriano and Masaccio to redecorate them. In these two men, at work in Rome about the same time in the 1420s, two utterly different worlds neared each other momentarily and then passed on. In the cosmopolitan Gothic of Gentile, the art of painting lingered nostalgically over the graceful dreams and fancies of the Middle Ages. With Masaccio it seemed to awake with a start from the sleep of centuries: man regained a stimulating consciousness of his powers and his privileged position in a world which now, at the dawn of the Renaissance, he was learning to see steadily and whole in relation to himself. But the Church was not yet aware of these two opposing outlooks or of any necessity of choosing between them.

Nor did Martin's successor, Eugenius IV, really face the issue and take sides, though he has been regarded as a determined advocate of Humanism. During his pontificate such artists as Donatello, Brunelleschi, Michelozzo and Rossellino were active in Rome; at his court a number of humanists gathered and found employment. But men in power at that time patronized artists and scholars almost as a matter of course; and while the pope followed suit, his spiritual allegiance was with the past, not with the new age. Like Martin V, Eugenius IV sponsored an art of courtly refinement seen

FILARETE (C. 1400-1469?): BRONZE DOOR AT THE MAIN ENTRANCE OF ST PETER'S, 1433-1445.

at its best in fine goldwork. He continued to rely on pomp and display to uphold the prestige of the Church, throwing as it were a glittering veil over the intrigues and vacillations that were undermining its authority. Like his predecessor, Eugenius IV commissioned a splendid gold mitre, inset with pearls and precious stones, from the most famous goldsmith and sculptor of the day, Lorenzo Ghiberti. It was Ghiberti who designed and cast the second bronze door of the Florentine Baptistery, a work the pope had seen and admired. So it was probably not by chance that Eugenius IV called on one of Ghiberti's assistants, Antonio Averlino, known as Filarete, to execute the most ambitious art project of his pontificate: the bronze door of St Peter's.

Filarete cuts a singular figure in Renaissance art history, standing somewhat apart from his contemporaries, unattached to any particular movement. Schooled in Florence, he spent many years in Rome (c. 1433-1455) where, as Vasari tells us, Filarete and his assistants "toiled twelve years" to complete the bronze door of St Peter's. Though in Rome, with the passage of time, he steeped himself in classical culture, actually his interest in classicism was sporadic and unsubstantial; it savours of mere curiosity rather than moral conviction; it is not based on an historical conception of classical art. Filarete gave Eugenius the very thing the pope probably wanted: a work rich and brilliant, anecdotal and erudite, a studied compound of classicism and Christianity based on the typically medieval concept of the perennial, inexhaustible continuity of classicism. The humanists, on the other hand, by the very fact that they aspired to a rebirth of classicism, recognized it as an interrupted movement of thought objectively remote from their own time; in other words they clearly perceived its historical limits.

In the very year in which Filarete set to work on his bronze door, Donatello was in Rome and undoubtedly gave him advice and suggestions. But while Donatello's flat, depressed relief was a means of succinctly conveying perspective and spatial recession, the flattening of Filarete's figures against the ground plane merely reveals a predilection for surfaces—surfaces teeming with ornamentation and highly diversified by means of continuously unfolding but rather unimaginative accents. Over the dense network of minute clefts and ridges, light plays and ricochets in broken gleams. The two bronze leaves of the door were originally gilt, at least in part, thus enhancing the richness of their effect.

The general conception of the door, in keeping with these purely surface effects, answers to no particular structural purpose. Space here is not rhythmically patterned, as it had been in Ghiberti's doors for the Florentine Baptistery, even though the latter was not committed to a vision of the fully developed Renaissance type. But Ghiberti's doors, with their clear-cut partitions, at least create a sharp distinction between the external setting and the internal space which appears to be contained within the surrounding architectural framework; they are conceived, in other words, in relation to that architectonic space. Filarete's door, on the contrary, is free of any reference to its setting; it is like a tapestry hung over the opening of the doorway. The two leaves of the door fit together perfectly to form a single plane. The spiralling plant designs surrounding the six main panels subdue the salience of their relief; they neither quicken the surface nor, with their slow and stately convolutions, do they generate any energy.

The diffuse inertness of the conception, together with the painstaking execution, adds to the ostentation and anecdotal variety of the work a curiously severe and solemn effect well suited to its demonstrative purpose and erudite character. This demonstrative purpose may well reflect the increasing concern felt by the pope over the dissension between the Greek and Roman Churches. For Eugenius IV was sparing no effort to reunite the two Churches and to consolidate his own position as the sole and undisputed authority of all Christendom—a prerogative substantiated by the Church's claim to be the heir of ancient Rome (again the medieval concept of the *ecclesia imperialis* dear to Boniface VIII). It so happens that the two panels representing the martyrdom of St Peter and St Paul, located beneath the full-length figures of the two Apostles, contain a wealth of topographical details and other particulars insistently alluding to Imperial Rome: armour, labara, shields, medallions and buildings. All round the six main panels, among the ornamental designs, are tiny episodes drawn from classical mythology and Roman history: Leda and the swan, Ganymede carried off by Zeus, Romulus and Remus, etc.

Throughout, the artist has made a point of emphasizing the parallel between the sovereign prestige of ancient Rome and that of papal Rome—a parallel borne out not only by geography and topography, but by history as well. For the history of the early martyrs, the "ancients" of the Church, is closely interwoven with that of the Roman Empire. The martyrdom of the Apostles effected a kind of blood transfusion from ancient Rome to Christian Rome. Here then, in Filarete's bronze door, the medieval concept of the unbroken continuity of classicism is taken up and reformulated with a precise intention. But the artist was not really interested in classical art for its own sake; even in his choice of style he makes no distinction between Imperial and Early Christian Rome. Thus we find him borrowing indiscriminately from Trajan's Column (i.e. from a spurious form of classicism, actually closer to Late Roman art and, by the same token, to Early Christian art) and from the doors of Early Christian basilicas (from which derives the continuous, unpunctuated sequence of the panels); indeed, in this combination, we can almost feel the artist seeking for the point at which the two styles merge.

When the Council of Florence adjourned in 1439, a general agreement had been reached between the Pope and the Patriarch of Constantinople: the primacy of the Pope was recognized by all and a decree was read in public uniting the Greek and

FILARETE (C. 1400-1469?): EUGENIUS IV RECEIVING THE KEYS FROM ST PETER, DETAIL OF THE BRONZE DOOR OF ST PETER'S.

51

DONATELLO (C. 1386-1466) AND MICHELOZZO (1396-1472): TABERNACLE OF THE SACRAMENT, 1432-1433. MARBLE.
CAPPELLA DEI BENEFICIATI IN ST PETER'S.

Roman Churches under his authority. Filarete, then at work on his bronze door, added in the horizontal bands between the main panels some small scenes representing the most memorable episodes of the Council. For the successful conclusion of the Council was the crowning achievement of that policy of Christian unity which Eugenius IV had so whole-heartedly pursued, and with which, as indicated above, the conception of the door of St Peter's was evidently associated.

The residence of the popes during the Middle Ages had been the old Lateran Palace, where the Empress Fausta had lived in the days of Constantine the Great. The ancient building had been continually enlarged and embellished until the popes left Rome for Avignon. Gregory XI, who brought the papacy back to Rome in 1377, was the first pope to reside in the Vatican, in a building begun by Eugenius III (1145-1153); but Gregory died before he had had time to remodel it to any great extent. The first substantial additions were made by Boniface IX (1389-1404), followed by Eugenius IV and Nicholas V. The latter engaged Leon Battista Alberti not only to rebuild the Vatican Palace but to redesign and embellish the whole Vatican City. "He erected," wrote Vespasiano da Bisticci of Nicholas V, "such a building as would have been fit not only for a pope, but for one of those Roman emperors who ruled the whole world." Of this extensive complex, girdled by a wall fortified with large round towers, we can still form an idea from old prints and drawings. Of what remains we shall have something to say presently: the old library, the room turned into a chapel by Nicholas V, the rooms on the first floor that became the Borgia Apartment, and the rooms or *stanze* on the second floor later frescoed by Raphael.

Inside the palace, on the site of an earlier Chapel of St Nicholas, Eugenius IV had founded a pontifical chapel dedicated to the Holy Sacrament; designed and built by the architect Bernardo Rossellino, it was demolished about 1540 to make way for new constructions. In all probability Donatello's Tabernacle of the Sacrament, now in St Peter's, was originally designed for this chapel. The work was carried out in 1432-1433 when Donatello was in Rome with his friend Michelozzo, who also had a share in it; for the style of the two groups of angels at the base of the tabernacle plainly shows them to be by Michelozzo. Thus in the same year in which Filarete was beginning the bronze door of St Peter's, another work was being produced, very different in conception, which marked a genuine innovation and pointed the way to the future; whereas the pseudo-humanistic conception of Filarete's work definitely harked back to the past. The contrast now between Filarete and Donatello was not unlike that between Gentile da Fabriano and Masaccio in the time of Martin V.

Donatello did not aim at showy or fanciful effects, he was unconcerned with erudition or the mere commemoration of events. Instead he went straight to the heart of his theme, dwelling on its human interest and bringing out the play of feelings in all their dramatic vitality and immediacy. There is nothing bookish or pedantic about his humanism, it does not consist of retrospects and reminiscences but is the direct expression of a surging, almost boisterous force exalting man's most passionate energies and almost violently laying bare his new features. Donatello's humanity is warmer and more immediate than that of Masaccio, with whom he has much in common: it is more open and expansive, at times more tremulous and impalpable, hence more refined, yet on the whole of a more popular order. The space in which Donatello's figures live and move is not independent or self-contained, but exists only in terms of the action his figures are engaged in. We have already seen how Giotto conceived space, grandly and nobly, as a pre-existing entity with respect to the bodies which occupy it and which seem to find there the fixed and immutable laws of their being, as well as the limits of their actions. Donatello's space, on the other hand, brings bodies into relation with each other and interrelates their actions; indeed it arises from their mutual relationships, it is the outcome of their dramatic interaction. It is not a wall that shuts them in, but a mainspring that propels them.

From the radically flattened and contracted ground plane, this space dynamically thrusts itself forward, bringing the masses with it, infusing them with its own expanding force and driving power. Everything here is movement and dramatic energy. True, there is a gradation of perspective synthetically expressed, but this synthesis only serves to sum up and condense the process whereby space takes form and gathers momentum; it is not a static synthesis, manifesting itself like a metaphysical occurrence, such as we find in Giotto. In this pre-eminently mobile conception light assumes paramount importance—light that is neither diffused uniformly within the picture space so as to take its abstract measure, nor broken up into distinct zones of light and shade so as to stress the rhythm of a preconceived, mentally defined space, but light that creates and expresses its dynamism and developments, flooding, caressing or lashing surfaces, like a wave that gently or roughly moulds the forms over which it sweeps.

This surge of light floods and models the whole upper part of the tabernacle. The architecture of the tabernacle, be it noted, is by no means designed in accordance with rigorous standards or harmoniously proportioned—which has been accounted a shortcoming, almost a barbarism, by those who have failed to grasp the life-force that this architecture expresses in its rugged strength and in the vigour of its projecting surfaces. Note for example, in the upper part, how in order to sharpen the separation between the front pilasters and the ones behind, Donatello carved the two angels in the rear in much lower relief, while those in front, drawing the curtain behind which the Entombment of Christ is being enacted, are almost carved in the round. The Entombment scene is thus projected vigorously outward, towards the spectator. This forward thrust is further emphasized by the deep recession immediately beneath it, forming an empty space occupied only by the pediment and two recumbent *putti*. Below, in the two groups of angels at the base of the pilasters, we find the same contrast between the slighter, flatter relief of the rearward figures and the more fully rounded

DONATELLO (C. 1386-1466): THE ENTOMBMENT, DETAIL OF THE TABERNACLE OF THE SACRAMENT, 1432-1433. CAPPELLA DEI BENEFICIATI IN ST PETER'S.

forms of those in front. Here, it is safe to say, the design is still Donatello's, but the execution reveals the less delicate hand of Michelozzo. Logically enough, Donatello confined the heavier, more static work of his companion to that part of the tabernacle whose structural inertia is greatest; for the essential function of the two lower groups of angels is to provide sturdy support for the massive structure above.

Succeeding Eugenius IV in 1447, Nicholas V differed from his predecessors in warmly and unreservedly espousing the cause of Humanism. He threw open the doors of the Vatican to scholars and artists, patronizing them lavishly. The first pope to grasp the scope and importance of that great ferment of ideas, he must have realized that the only way for the Church to contain the forces at work and neutralize their secular impact was to assimilate their outward forms. He must have realized too how greatly

FRA ANGELICO (C. 1400-1455): FRESCOES IN THE CHAPEL OF NICHOLAS V, 1447-1449.

56

the prestige of the Church would be enhanced if the Vatican, the centre of the Faith, could also become the centre of art and learning—but art and learning set free, as the humanists stipulated, from the shackles that had bound medieval art and science. It was of course in the Church's interest to control and influence the new culture in the making, and to do so from within.

Nicholas V therefore did his utmost to place the Vatican in the forefront of the revival of classical literature, learning and art. He practically founded the Vatican Library. Inheriting about three hundred and forty volumes, most of them acquired by Eugenius IV (only a small part of the precious store of manuscripts gathered together by the popes in the Middle Ages had survived), he left behind him several thousand. He sent his agents all over Europe, from England to Athens and Constantinople, to buy or copy Greek and Latin manuscripts. He restored many monuments, sacred and profane alike, and carried out a vast building programme in the Vatican. He patronized famous artists (Leon Battista Alberti, Piero della Francesca, Andrea del Castagno) and famous scholars and men of letters (Poggio, Lorenzo Valla, Marsilio Ficino). He called in Fra Angelico to decorate the chapel bearing his name with a fresco cycle of scenes from the lives of St Stephen and St Lawrence, painted between 1447 and 1449. In the career of the great Tuscan master these frescoes mark a turning point, almost a fresh statement of aims, which was undoubtedly due in large measure to the influence exerted on him by the humanist milieu of the papal court and probably in part to the ideological directives of the pope himself.

The legend given currency by Vasari has woven a halo of saintliness round the pious figure of Fra Angelico, the Angelic Brother, who lived the quiet life of a Dominican monk and is supposed to have painted in a state of religious ecstasy, reproducing his mystical visions. In actual fact, the painting of Fra Angelico reveals a profound doctrinal rigour and a keen awareness of the problems it raises. He too was a man of the Renaissance and acquiesced in its cultural climate; the great formative influence on his art was that of Masaccio. But a vivid personality and deep-seated religious convictions led him to take up a peculiar position: his participation in humanist culture was profoundly controversial, his attitude to secular trends of thought serenely but obstinately polemical. To the rationalism of Brunelleschi, the subjective dramatization of Masaccio and Donatello, and the courtliness of Alberti, he opposed a kind of

The frescoed chamber now known as the Cappella Niccolina, or the Chapel of Nicholas V, originally formed part of a tower built in the opening years of the thirteenth century and later incorporated in the new Vatican residence built by Pope Nicholas III about 1278. It was converted into a chapel by Nicholas V, who had it entirely decorated by Fra Angelico. Executed between 1447 and 1449, the frescoes illustrate episodes in the lives of St Lawrence and St Stephen. The marble pavement, bearing the signs of the zodiac and the name of Nicholas V, is the work of the Florentine artist Agnolo Verrone.

FRA ANGELICO (C. 1400-1455): ST LAWRENCE DISTRIBUTING ALMS, 1447-1449. CHAPEL OF NICHOLAS V.

TEMPLA DOMVM EXPOSITIS·VICOS·FORA·MOENIA·PONTES·
VIRGINEAM·TRIVII·QVOD·REPARARIS·AQVAM·
PRISCA·LICET·NAVTIS·STATVAS·DARE·COMMODA·PORTVS·
ET·VATICANVM·CINGERE·SIXTE·IVGVM·
PLVS·TAMEN·VRBS·DEBET·NAM·QVAE·SQVALORE·LATEBAT·
CERNITVR·IN·CELEBRI·BIBLIOTHECA·LOCO·

MELOZZO DA FORLÌ (1438-1494): SIXTUS IV APPOINTING PLATINA VATICAN LIBRARIAN, ABOUT 1477. PINACOTECA VATICANA.

idealism which, while recapturing the spirit of medieval mysticism, re-expressed it in humanistic terms. Thus his work is at once novel and traditional. He accepted the new proportions of Renaissance space, with its crystalline clarity of definition which denotes the powers of the mind being brought to bear on the vision of reality, in contrast to a passive, "revealed," purely mystical perception of reality. But with Fra Angelico this limpidity of mind, elevated to a level of ideal purity, led directly to God. His vision has none of the rapt or reckless accents of ecstasy, but those rather of the serene meditations of a privileged intercessor between Nature and God. Here is an artist engaged not in the pure contemplation of God, but in a demonstration of His existence—a demonstration summed up in the light that pervades his space and makes colours glow like gems, hymning the beauty of all created things.

In the frescoes in the Chapel of Nicholas V, Fra Angelico seems to confront the problem of Renaissance classicism and to define his attitude towards it more clearly than in any previous work. Filarete, as noted above, had already sought to localize the point of junction between the style of Imperial Rome and that of Christian Rome, with a view to demonstrating the unbroken continuity of classicism and the legitimacy of the Church's claim to the heritage of ancient Rome; by doing so he reverted to a medieval conception and so remained on the fringe of Humanism. Fra Angelico, on the other hand (and here we may perhaps discern the effect of the new cultural policy steadily pursued from Eugenius IV to Nicholas V), acted in accordance with the ideas and principles of Humanism. Unlike Filarete, he had a distinct, history-conscious conception of classicism and Latinity; and he looked for a counterweight to this idea in an equally high and august conception of Christianity, equally justified by history. As G.C. Argan has observed, the martyr saints Stephen and Lawrence are seen by Fra Angelico in the guise of "ancients" of the Church, much as Filarete had seen Peter and Paul on the bronze doors of St Peter's. Their actions take place in settings appropriate to the historical dignity of the narrative. History, in the humanist acceptation of the term, is a sense of the remoteness of the past coupled with an intense and vivid recollection of it. Such a sense of dim remoteness and vivid presence was conjured up now in the frescoes of Fra Angelico, in the stately gravity of the compositions, in the severer dimensions and more subdued solemnity of his architecture, in the accent of nobility pervading the luminous clarity of the design. Even though Benozzo Gozzoli had a hand in the work, the underlying unity of this fresco cycle remains unimpaired.

The Vatican picture gallery, or Pinacoteca, founded early in the nineteenth century, includes many works which, having entered the collections in recent times and thus having no direct connection with the history of the Vatican, have gone unmentioned in this book. Of particular interest and importance is the group of Quattrocento paintings, one of the finest of which is the *Pietà* of Giovanni Bellini, which once formed part of the great altarpiece executed for the church of San Francesco at Pesaro.

GIOVANNI BELLINI (C. 1430-1516): PIETÀ, ABOUT 1475. FROM THE CHURCH OF SAN FRANCESCO AT PESARO. PINACOTECA VATICANA.

The triumph of the new culture promoted by Nicholas V seemed to be ensured by the election of Aeneas Sylvius Piccolomini, who took the name of Pius II (1458-1464). A highly cultivated man with brilliant gifts, diplomatist and statesman, Latinist, orator, poet and a voluminous writer, he was an eminent humanist in his own right. As such, however, he foresaw the dangers and complications ahead, and instead of adopting a conciliatory policy towards Humanism, as Nicholas V had done, he tried to bring it under the strict control of the papacy. But he patronized the arts and even embarked on a large-scale building programme in Pienza, his native town. His major undertaking in the Vatican was the loggia for the papal benediction in front of St Peter's, which disappeared with the demolition of the old basilica. Extending his cultural activities throughout Europe, he helped to found and endow the universities

Clearly visible in this drawing by the Dutch painter Maerten van Heemskerck is the Loggia delle Benedizioni, built under Pius II (1458-1464) and abutting on the portico of Old St Peter's. On the upper right are the Loggie, the open galleries decorated by Raphael; this arcaded façade, designed by Bramante and Raphael for Julius II (1503-1513), was subsequently incorporated, under Gregory XIII (1572-1585) and Sixtus V (1585-1590), in the buildings round the present Court of St Damasus.

MAERTEN VAN HEEMSKERCK (1498-1574): DRAWING OF OLD ST PETER'S AND THE VATICAN PALACES. ABOUT 1533. ALBERTINA, VIENNA.

of Nantes, Ingolstadt and Basel. Himself an extraordinarily versatile writer (he wrote fiction, essays, memoirs, histories, travel sketches and even a comedy), he loved fine books for their own sake. Rome by now was Italy's leading centre (after Venice) of book production, and during his pontificate the binder's art flourished there as never before, chiefly under the influence of Oriental and German bindings. The Vatican Library contains a posthumous edition of the *Epistolae* of Pope Pius II which is also a superlative example of fine book-making, with its gorgeous yet sober and robust binding, executed at Nuremberg in 1481 for Cardinal Francesco Piccolomini.

The first printed book to appear in Italy was published at Subiaco in 1465. In Rome the first printing press went into operation in 1467, in the pontificate of Paul II (1464-1471), one of whose principal merits lay in encouraging the diffusion of printing. With Paul II, however, the progress of the Renaissance marked a temporary pause. Though himself a scholar, he was profoundly mistrustful of the humanist circles in Rome and their paganizing spirit. After the short-lived attempt of Nicholas V, implemented by Fra Angelico's frescoes, to assimilate the ideals of Humanism to those of Christianity and thus to exert a shaping influence on the new culture from within, the tactics adopted by Pius II, of subjecting Humanism to the authority of the papacy, proved for a time to be a shrewd and effective policy. But the peremptory and intransigent reaction of Paul II is readily understandable. The dream of reconciling Christianity with the classical world was fondly entertained by some of the greatest minds of the age, from Marsilio Ficino to Vittorino da Feltre and Pico della Mirandola. But all too often the gap between them could only be bridged by a compromise unsatisfactory to both. While profoundly religious men like Savonarola met every deviation from the strait way with fiery denunciations and lurid prophecies of future retribution, in official circles there arose an *entente*, a reciprocal though superficial respect and toleration between the two ideological spheres. All paid homage and professed submission to the Church, though in many cases it was only lip-service. Lay morality in the early phase of Humanism can scarcely be called strict, but had, rather, a hedonistic savour of neo-paganism. The innovating spirit of the Renaissance, moreover, affected—not to say loosened—the manners and morals of the high clergy and planted the seeds of free thought and worldliness at the papal court. Another source of trouble and anxiety for the Church was the defence of the Papal States and the frontiers of the Vatican against aggressive neighbours. The papacy was thus involved in a web of political scheming and a steadily corroding conflict of temporal interests that not only sapped its energies but lowered its prestige.

This was the atmosphere in which the successor of Paul II, Sixtus IV (1471-1484), ascended the papal throne. A lavish patron of the arts and of humanist culture generally, Sixtus gave fresh impetus to the architectural embellishment of Rome and to historical studies. He surrounded himself with scholars and men of letters. He reopened the Roman Academy of Pomponius Laetus, which Paul II had closed and disbanded;

and he rehabilitated Platina, a leading humanist persecuted and imprisoned by Paul II. In 1475 Platina was put in charge of the Vatican Library, which under Sixtus was signally enlarged and enriched. It was this appointment that inspired the famous fresco by Melozzo da Forlì, executed about 1477; originally adorning the walls of the old library, it is now in the Pinacoteca Vaticana. Platina is shown kneeling before the pope; standing behind them, from left to right, are Giovanni della Rovere, prefect of Rome, Girolamo Riario, future governor of Forlì, Cardinal Giuliano della Rovere (the future Pope Julius II) and Raffaele Riario, protonotary apostolic. The scene is imbued with festive solemnity. The facial features of the figures are magisterially portrayed, with almost sculpturesque precision. The splendour and vastness of the architectural setting, all in blue and gold, enhances, with its majestic proportions, the ceremonial magnificence of the scene.

Melozzo, one of the favourite painters of Sixtus IV, paid homage in this work to the enlightened patron of the humanists, expressing something of their reverence for the papal power. But apart from this commemorative purpose, no particular ideological import is apparent. The elements of the style and technique are those handed down by the creators of Quattrocento Italian art: Masaccio, Piero della Francesca, Leon Battista Alberti. But the uses to which they are put here are already substantially different. While applying the rules of perspective with great skill, Melozzo no longer thinks out the problems of space; instead of visualizing it by an effort of his own imagination and mastering its implications to the full, he merely transcribes a solution already worked out by others. Not for him the dramatic intensity of Masaccio, the transcendental abstractions of Piero, the illuminated idealism of Fra Angelico. His classicism no longer springs from a profound, self-experienced consciousness of history; Melozzo is no historian, but a charming chronicler. True, he aspires to expand the chronicle into history, but the attempt remains unsuccessful.

A certain concern with portraiture was inseparable from this attempt. The synthetic character of early Quattrocento portraits had given place to an analytical character; idealism had given place to realism. Artists sought to portray their subjects true to life, rendering features acutely, with an eye for telling details, almost subordinating style to lifelikeness, instead of regarding style as an absolute to which only idealized, transcendentalized figures could suitably conform. Portraiture now, in the latter part of the fifteenth century, began to flourish as an independent art form (Melozzo's fresco is evidence of this), its development going hand in hand with that of narrative painting, dealing in lively and colourful terms with everyday life, which accordingly gave rise to such gifted artists as Domenico Ghirlandaio, and others of slender resources but shrewdly observant like Cosimo Rosselli.

These two painters had a large share—though not an outstanding one artistically— in the major art project undertaken in the Vatican by Sixtus IV: the fresco decorations

"EPISTOLAE" OF POPE PIUS II, BINDING EXECUTED AT NUREMBERG IN 1481. VATICAN LIBRARY.

of the Sistine Chapel (1481-1483). While their participation calls for no particular comment, it certainly harmonized well with the prevailing character of the fresco cycle as a whole: its gracious, free and easy narrative style, unfolding continuously over the wall surface in a rhythmically articulated sequence of scenes. Until Michelangelo (in 1536-1541) covered the back wall with his great vision of the Last Judgement, thus blotting out the earlier paintings there, the long band of Quattrocento frescoes extended round the entire perimeter of the chapel, like a window thrown open on an unbroken succession of smiling landscapes and majestic buildings. The concise and pregnant space of Giotto and Masaccio had been supplanted by the panoramic view, and intensity by expansiveness.

The architecture of the new palace chapel (built to the order of Sixtus IV about 1475, perhaps by Baccio Pontelli, on the site of an earlier chapel) was well in keeping with the character of the decorations. It forms a single spacious hall, 130 feet long, 44 feet wide and 65 feet high; seen from the outside (later constructions now block the view), it has the shape of a regular parallelepiped, its outer walls as bare as those of a fortress. The great cube of the interior, rounded off overhead by an elegant vault originally painted blue and gold in imitation of the night sky, aimed at an effect of sacramental solemnity, but failed to achieve any well-defined spatial quality. Rather than space we should perhaps speak of ambience, of a ceremonial atmosphere where clouds of incense floated up, choirs reverberated, conclaves sat and solemn gatherings deliberated; where the eye ranges freely in light evenly diffused by the high windows. The law of this space, which neither seeks nor finds any peculiar intensity of its own, being defined solely in terms of its regular development, consists in the rhythmic convergence of the elements enclosing it and the symmetrical correspondence of wall to wall, window to window, lunette to lunette.

The same regularity governs the distribution of the frescoes. The two cycles with episodes from the lives of Christ (to the left of the altar) and Moses (to the right) figured—before Michelangelo set to work—on the two short walls of the chapel, the successive scenes of the first cycle symmetrically corresponding with those of the second. The question therefore arises whether this carefully devised symmetry, self-evident in the design of the chapel and the layout of the decorations, may not have served an ulterior purpose. It is reasonable to suppose that it did. It was intended to emphasize parallel episodes in the two fresco cycles representing the lives of Moses and Christ (for example, *Moses giving the Rod to Joshua* and *Christ giving the Keys to St Peter*), in keeping with a theme that was common in medieval iconography: the "concordance" between the Old and the New Testament. "*Moises noster Christus*" (Our Moses is Christ), wrote Sixtus IV in one of his theological works. The method is that of the "parallel lives" of Plutarch, following the ancient rhetorical principle whereby the conjunction of two terms is the most effective way of stressing both their similarities and their differences, thus conducing to a better understanding of each.

THE INTERIOR OF THE SISTINE CHAPEL AS IT APPEARED IN THE FIFTEENTH CENTURY.
RECONSTRUCTION BY G. TOGNETTI.

Above, looking towards the altar, is the Sistine Chapel as it must have appeared at the end of the fifteenth
century, before Michelangelo frescoed the ceiling and painted his *Last Judgement* behind the altar, sealing up
the two windows, and covering over the Quattrocento frescoes on the back wall. The original ceiling, as shown
here, was painted in blue and dotted with golden stars. In simulated niches beside the windows are represented
thirty of the early popes, nearly all of them martyrs. In the middle section of the wall are the main panels
with scenes from the lives of Moses and Christ. Beneath them are painted draperies. The marble choir screen,
carved by Mino da Fiesole, who also designed the *cantoria* or singing gallery, to the right of it, served to divide
the chancel from the congregation, in accordance with the liturgical usage of the Middle Ages. The pavement
is inlaid with stones of different colours.

LUCA SIGNORELLI (C. 1441-1523) AND ASSISTANTS: MOSES GIVING THE ROD TO JOSHUA, 1482.
FRESCO IN THE SISTINE CHAPEL.

It would be a mistake to suppose that this implied reference to Plutarch was merely accidental. For of all the authors of pagan antiquity he and Plato were regarded as having most in common with Christian thought and ethics, and as being the most likely intermediaries between classicism and Christianity—in other words, between Humanism and religion. It was to Plutarch that Vittorino da Feltre, perhaps the greatest teacher and educator of the Renaissance, turned in his attempt to reconcile the classical tradition and humanist ideals with the Christian life; and it was in the school of Vittorino da Feltre that Platina was trained, the favourite of Sixtus IV and author of the inscriptions accompanying the pictures of the early popes painted by Ghirlandaio, Cosimo Rosselli and Botticelli between the windows of the Sistine Chapel.

Therefore, the theme of "parallel lives" developed in the Sistine Chapel should perhaps be construed in larger terms as an endorsement of Plutarch's ethical ideals, which had been revived and put into practice in humanist circles, by Vittorino da Feltre in particular: self-control, peace of mind, harmonious development of the personality,

PERUGINO (C. 1445-1523): CHRIST GIVING THE KEYS TO ST PETER, 1482.
FRESCO IN THE SISTINE CHAPEL.

physical health and mental discipline, equilibrium and order, mildness and kindliness, taken as the standard of the moral life and as the supreme virtues. These aspirations, moreover, were consistent with the revival of naturalism in art, for they could apply that naturalism (also fostered by the hedonistic neo-paganism that had caused Paul II so much anxiety) to a Christian vision. Above and beyond the dramatic moral earnestness that had marked the work of men like Masaccio and Donatello, this new aspiration towards serenity and harmony seems particularly appropriate to the general purport conveyed by the stylistic characteristics of the Sistine Chapel: nature seen as a blithe and pleasure-giving spectacle, and order and equilibrium embodied in an ideal symmetry.

But the personality best suited to interpreting this aspiration seems to have been that of Pietro Vannucci, better known as Perugino, an Umbrian painter who also had a share in the Sistine frescoes alongside his Tuscan colleagues Sandro Botticelli and Luca Signorelli, and the above-mentioned Ghirlandaio and Rosselli. In the scene of

SANDRO BOTTICELLI (1445-1510): THE PURIFICATION OF THE LEPER AND THE TEMPTATION OF CHRIST, 1481-1482.
FRESCO IN THE SISTINE CHAPEL.

Christ giving the Keys to St Peter, for which Perugino was responsible, the composition is faultlessly balanced. Its symmetry answers to an ideal of harmony well realized here in the suavity of the landscape, the graceful cadence of the figure grouping, the subtle gradations of light and colour. Perugino's limitations lie precisely in this bland and languid grace of his, in this monotonously balanced distribution of the picture elements which—though in this case it squares with the architecture of the chapel—robs his perspective of any power of spatial synthesis. But his spiritual outlook is important because it prepared the way for the new aesthetic of Raphael.

Perugino was Raphael's master, and Signorelli was Michelangelo's. To the Tuscans, to Pollaiolo especially, Signorelli owed the harsh and masculine force of his design. His linework is tense and sinewy, his volumes full-bodied and well articulated. In the famous frescoes in the Chapel of San Brizio in the cathedral of Orvieto, painted between 1492 and 1502, he rose to unprecedented heights of dramatic brio. But in the Sistine Chapel, in a scene from the life of Moses, he refrains from violence and tumult.

SANDRO BOTTICELLI (1445-1510): SCENES FROM THE LIFE OF MOSES, 1481-1482.
FRESCO IN THE SISTINE CHAPEL.

He is robust but not harsh; his figure groups, unfolding with a fluent, unbroken rhythm, are ordered and symmetrical as never before. Landscape is unusually rich in narrative notations. There may be several reasons for this: the fact that this is a work preceding his full maturity, and also the fairly large share his assistants had in it (Bartolomeo della Gatta above all). But the chief reason is certainly that Signorelli had to abide by the general conception of the chapel and of the other frescoes, whose whole tenor is one of spacious, undramatic equilibrium and serenely naturalistic story-telling.

The naturalistic and narrative treatment of landscape, required of all participants in the work, is a predominant feature of the frescoes executed by Botticelli who, like Signorelli, was not interested in landscape for its own sake. This is evidenced by his painting and incidentally confirmed by a passage in Leonardo's *Treatise on Painting*: "One who cares not for landscapes looks upon them as a matter of brief and simple investigation, as when our Botticelli said that such study was vain, for merely throwing

SANDRO BOTTICELLI (1445-1510): SCENES FROM THE LIFE OF MOSES, DETAIL OF THE EXODUS, 1481-1482. FRESCO IN THE SISTINE CHAPEL.

a sponge dipped in divers colours against a wall leaves thereon a stain in which a fine landscape can be seen." With Botticelli (as already to some extent with Pollaiolo) perspective lost its function of relating bodies with space. Figures are no longer integrated in a definite spatial setting; emerging from a purely allusive space wholly absorbed by the background, they stand forth in the crystal clarity and musicality of their linear design. Like extracts or essences of space, they move in a kind of void, the dimension best befitting their emotional detachment, their lyrical and fantastic aloofness. In the Sistine Chapel, however, in the *Purification of the Leper*, Botticelli was called upon to create a landscape setting crowded with figures, trees, rocks and buildings. He marshalled his figures into two files beginning at each extremity of the composition and curving inward towards the centre background, thus suggesting an unlimited perspective and throwing back the vanishing point towards the receding arcades of the Quattrocento façade. Once he had created these conditions, he could give free play to a sweeping, flexuous rhythm of lines, undefined in space, almost like a broad flutter of wings. In the fresco representing scenes from the life of Moses (from the slaying of the Egyptian on the right to the Exodus on the left), the figure groups are alternately massed and scattered, and it is this uneven distribution that gives its meaning to the dispersion of space. The linework, whether tensed or delicately flexed, everywhere performs the function of detaching the figures from the setting. Faces convey the psychological expression of that detachment, as if a screen were interposed between the inner world of these self-absorbed men and women and the outer world they have to cope with.

Botticelli's aesthetic is far removed from the neo-Plutarchian and Catholic ideals of Perugino. It has its roots in a world of wayward, faintly melancholy dreams— the dreams of one who seems to be looking back to the classical age, to its paganism and mythology, with wistful regret, as if yearning for a remembered state of lost happiness. But this nostalgia, acting on the conscience of a sincere Christian, gave rise to a latent sense of guilt, and this explains the deflection of his vision towards the pathetic, conscience-stricken accents of his later work, when the smooth curves of his line had turned into contorted spirals and obsessive swirls. These were the years of Savonarola's martyrdom (1498) and the pontificate of Alexander VI, the years too when Signorelli was painting his dramatic *Last Judgement* in Orvieto Cathedral.

Botticelli's exquisite drawings illustrating scenes from the *Divine Comedy*, of which several are preserved in the Vatican Library, represent a phase of his art immediately preceding his so-called "Piagnone" period (from the name given to Savonarola's followers). The works of a poet like Petrarch would surely have been more congenial to the lyrical vein and rhythmic grace characteristic of Botticelli's best pictures. But the moral austerity of Dante had an irresistible appeal for him. He admittedly failed to identify his style with the spirit of Dante's poetry; but he conjured up a haunting vision, wistful and ethereal, of a Paradise of his own, and another, not

SANDRO BOTTICELLI (1445-1510): ILLUSTRATION FOR DANTE'S DIVINE COMEDY, INFERNO, CANTO X:
THE FIERY TOMBS OF THE EPICUREAN HERETICS, DETAIL. VATICAN LIBRARY.

fearful and convulsive but subtly tormenting, of the Inferno. His swift and thread-like
line quivers with suppressed excitement. All that is vagrant and mercurial in his
vision seems here to materialize and remain for a moment in restless suspension.

The Sistine Chapel was inaugurated on the fifteenth of August 1483. A year later Sixtus IV died and was succeeded by Innocent VIII (1484-1492), who continued to patronize artists and beautify Rome. It was during his pontificate that Antonio Pollaiolo designed and cast the great tomb of Sixtus IV (1490-1493); after the death of Innocent VIII, he also executed this pope's tomb (1493-1497). Both of these funeral monuments have survived, the first in the Grotte Vaticane, the second in St Peter's. Donatello belonged to the first generation of the great Quattrocento Florentines, Botticelli to the third. Antonio Pollaiolo, painter, sculptor and goldsmith, represents the intervening generation. Taking his lead from Donatello, Filippo Lippi and above all Andrea del Castagno (with whom he had probably studied), he carried the principle of linearism to its uttermost consequences: the relentless vigour and excited accents of his outlines communicate a rugged energy and driving power to his figures. The image is recorded at the height of its tension, which galvanizes the surrounding space and inserts the figure in it. This is the tension, not of dramatic action, but of sheer vitality, of straining aspirations, of a burning need of unlimited expansion into nature, whose

ANTONIO POLLAIOLO (1432-1498): THE TOMB OF POPE SIXTUS IV, 1490-1493. BRONZE. VATICAN GROTTOES.

ANTONIO POLLAIOLO (1432-1498): BUST OF THE POPE, DETAIL OF THE TOMB OF SIXTUS IV.
BRONZE. VATICAN GROTTOES.

heart and soul is man, and into the history and myths of the classical past. But this vital impulse is filtered through the cerebral processes of abstract thought which characterize the first great achievements of Quattrocento Italian art. In Pollaiolo, therefore, we are not yet made aware of those undercurrents of naturalism and sensuality which rose to the surface in some of the artists of the next generation—but the psychological premises are there.

Through the magnificent sepulchral monument of Sixtus IV, cast in bronze, runs a continuous tremor which dramatically culminates in the pope's emaciated face.

The recumbent figure appears almost weightless, freed of bodily compulsions and absorbed in the luminous flux of the folds that wrinkle and furrow it, almost consumed and etherealized by the endless swirl of lines. The rich and intricate patterning of the pillows and draperies serves to intensify, to the utmost, the ever-shifting play of light that gives vitality to the surfaces. The tomb slab and the high base, admirably articulated in their contours and design, contribute to the same effect: in their breadth and sweep, and their succession of reliefs in highly compressed perspective, they blend with the light-drenched figure of the dead pope. The personifications of the Virtues and the Liberal Arts, set in panels round the slab and the base, rank among the most exquisite creations of fifteenth century Italian sculpture; Pollaiolo expresses himself here with an accent of grace and unruffled felicity momentarily free from the tensions of his visionary world.

ANTONIO POLLAIOLO (1432-1498): ALLEGORICAL FIGURE PERSONIFYING PHILOSOPHY.
BRONZE RELIEF, DETAIL OF THE TOMB OF SIXTUS IV. VATICAN GROTTOES.

DRAWING SHOWING THE TOMB OF INNOCENT VIII IN ITS ORIGINAL FORM. KUPFERSTICHKABINETT, BERLIN.

ANTONIO POLLAIOLO (1432-1498): THE TOMB OF POPE INNOCENT VIII, 1493-1497. NAVE OF ST PETER'S.

ANTONIO POLLAIOLO (1432-1498): THE POPE BLESSING, DETAIL OF THE TOMB OF INNOCENT VIII. NAVE OF ST PETER'S.

ANTONIO POLLAIOLO (1432-1498): RECUMBENT EFFIGY OF THE POPE, DETAIL OF THE TOMB OF INNOCENT VIII.
NAVE OF ST PETER'S.

The seventeenth century drawing on page 78 shows the Tomb of Innocent VIII in its original form, prior to the demolition of the nave of Old St Peter's. It reveals the fact that, when the monument was reassembled in the new church, the position of the two figures was reversed: the seated figure of the pope was originally placed below the recumbent effigy. In the course of the alterations, the monument also lost its original setting. In his left hand Innocent VIII is holding a relic of the Holy Lance, which had pierced the side of Christ on the Cross; this relic was presented to the pope in 1492, shortly before his death, by the Ottoman Sultan Bajazet II.

Less moving, but an equally arresting work, is the bronze tomb of Innocent VIII, whose unity was destroyed when the monument was disassembled and removed from Old St Peter's, then readapted to the new basilica. A contemporary drawing now in Berlin shows how it originally looked. The work is unusual in that the figure of the pope is represented twice: in life and in death, in the splendour of his pontificate and in eternal repose. It was precisely this contrast of the living man, at the height of his earthly power, with the chastening silence of death that stimulated Pollaiolo's imagination. Hence the fresh and vivid presence of the figure of Innocent VIII seated on the papal throne, his hand raised in blessing, in a rippling movement that seems like an anticipation of Baroque.

CEILING DECORATION IN THE BELVEDERE PALACE, ATTRIBUTED TO PIER MATTEO D'AMELIA.
NOW GALLERIA DEI BUSTI, VATICAN MUSEUMS.

PINTURICCHIO (1454-1513): THE MYTH OF ISIS AND OSIRIS AND THE ADORATION OF THE SACRED BULL APIS.
CEILING DECORATION IN THE SALA DEI SANTI, 1492-1495. BORGIA APARTMENT.

On a wooded hill near the papal residence Innocent VIII had a summer palace built, known as the Belvedere (on account of the view to be had from it), for which he commissioned frescoes from Mantegna, Pinturicchio and Bonfigli. It is a matter of regret that the chapel of the palace, frescoed by Mantegna, was destroyed under Pius VI (1775-1799) during the construction of the Museo Pio-Clementino, in which the Belvedere itself was incorporated.

All that now remains of the original decorations of the Belvedere are some lunettes and ceiling panels. One of the latter, attributed to the Umbrian painter Pier Matteo d'Amelia, shows a characteristic geometric pattern simulating a coffered ceiling, with ornamental Greek crosses disposed on either side of a large square containing in the centre the coat of arms of Innocent VIII. The form of the vaulted ceiling recalls that of the Sistine Chapel, which in fact was painted in blue and gold (the same colours as here) by the same artist, Pier Matteo d'Amelia.

The last pope of the fifteenth century was Alexander VI (1492-1503), *né* Rodrigo Borgia. He was the very embodiment of a worldly-minded, authoritarian pope wholly absorbed in temporal interests, and by no means of unimpeachable morals. With the accession of Alexander the union of Christianity and Humanism was made complete, anyhow on the aesthetic plane, where moral considerations were ignored or neutralized. Art became the direct expression of the wealth and power of the popes.

The frescoes executed by Pinturicchio and his assistants, from 1492 to 1495, in the private apartment remodelled and decorated by Alexander for his own use, and known as the Appartamento Borgia, answer perfectly to this courtly and luxurious conception of art. The apartment consists of six rooms, the grandest of which is the Sala dei Santi, where historical episodes are combined with allegorical themes, and Oriental and pagan myths with the lives of the Saints. Its splendour has none of the dazzling solemnity of the medieval tradition, but produces a joyful, festive effect. The colours are further enhanced with gilt ornamentation in relief, inserted within the pictorial design. The decoration extends to the ceilings, which are filled with small figures and friezes of gilt stucco, with medallions and coats of arms, like a gorgeous mantle spread overhead. The naturalistic and narrative schemes of the Sistine Chapel have here been transposed into a different key, no longer of serene equilibrium and pellucid harmony, but one rather of fabulous and exhilarating splendours.

In 1489, during the pontificate of Innocent VIII, there arrived in Rome the "Grand Turk," Prince Jem, who had been captured in Rhodes by the Knights of St John. This curious personage was the brother of the Ottoman Sultan Bajazet II (who paid the pope an annual tribute to keep Jem a close prisoner and so prevent him from pretending to the Turkish sultanate). The conspicuous figure of an Oriental in Pinturicchio's fresco of *St Catherine disputing with the Philosophers*, shown standing to the

VIEW OF THE SALA DEI SANTI IN THE BORGIA APARTMENT, WITH PINTURICCHIO'S FRESCOES
AND THE STALLS DECORATED WITH MARQUETRY.

PINTURICCHIO (1454-1513): PORTRAIT OF POPE ALEXANDER VI, DETAIL OF THE RESURRECTION, 1492-1495.
SALA DEI MISTERI DELLA FEDE, BORGIA APARTMENT.

PINTURICCHIO (1454-1513): ST CATHERINE OF ALEXANDRIA DISPUTING WITH THE PHILOSOPHERS BEFORE
THE EMPEROR MAXIMINUS, 1492-1495. SALA DEI SANTI, BORGIA APARTMENT.

A singular feature of Pinturicchio's frescoes in the Sala dei Santi is the combination of sacred subjects with mythological themes, of classical and even Oriental origin, in the triangular panels of the quadripartite vault. The large scene of *St Catherine disputing with the Philosophers before the Emperor Maximinus*, which occupies the large lunette of the wall opposite the window, also presents some iconographic peculiarities. The figure of the emperor seated on the throne has been identified—though not very plausibly—with Cesare Borgia, and the figure of the Saint with his sister Lucrezia. The man on the left, with a drooping moustache, is supposed to be a portrait of Andrew Palaeologus. Recognizable behind this personage are Antonio da Sangallo the Elder, holding a square, and Pinturicchio himself, a thin-faced figure with dark hair. The turbaned Oriental on the right is thought to represent Prince Jem, brother of the Turkish sultan and a prisoner of the pope's. In the right background stands the Arch of Constantine.

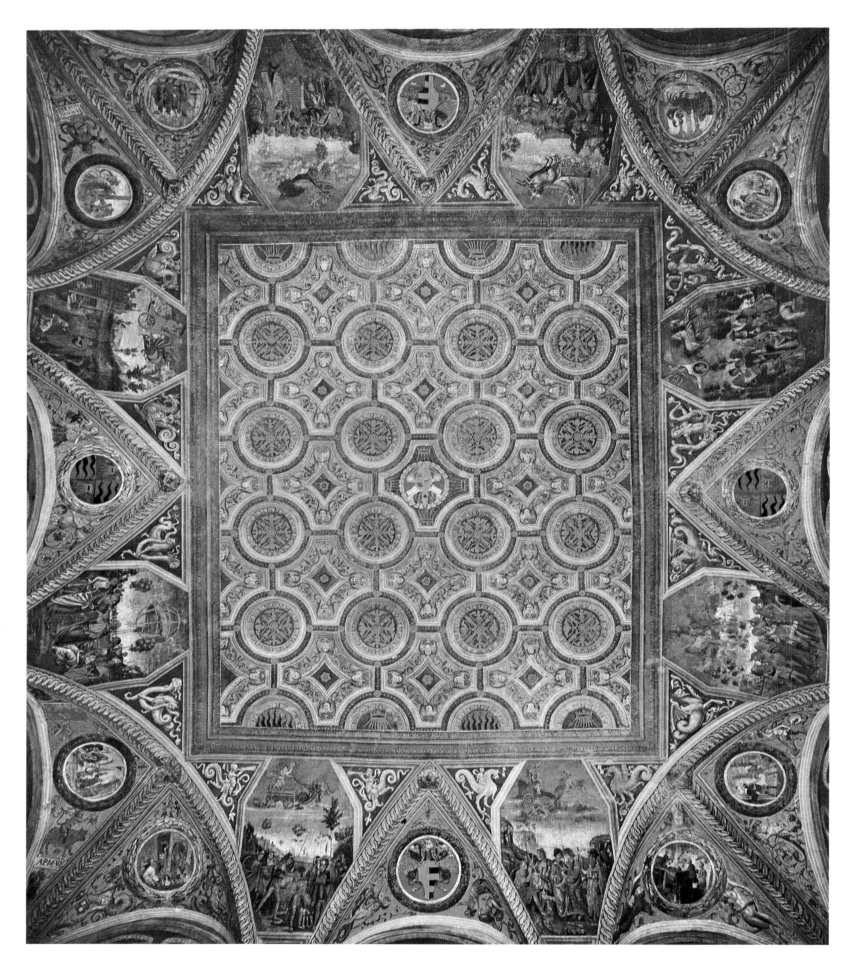

CEILING DECORATION PAINTED BY PINTURICCHIO'S ASSISTANTS. SALA DELLE SIBILLE, BORGIA APARTMENT.

right of the emperor, with arms akimbo, wearing a great white turban, is supposed to be a portrait of Prince Jem. In any case the gaudy Turkish costumes worn by this figure and his attendants must have been painted from life, for the artist has reproduced them accurately, and they contribute not a little to the exotic atmosphere to which these frescoes in the Borgia Apartment owe so much of their charm. The almost documentary verisimilitude with which Pinturicchio records details of costume, far from detracting from the fanciful and romantic character of the work, makes it all the more convincing as a glimpse of the fabled East, of the luxury-loving Moslem world. The colourful pageantry illustrated by Pinturicchio is actually but a reflection of day-to-day life as it was lived at the court of the prodigal, worldly-minded Borgia pope, Alexander VI.

LEONARDO DA VINCI (1452-1519): ST JEROME, ABOUT 1482. PINACOTECA VATICANA.

4

THE RECONSTRUCTION YEARS

Divested of the transcendental religious sentiments of the Middle Ages, early Quattrocento man had become conscious of himself as a responsible, free-thinking individual. This transition was not accomplished without dramatic tensions. But the confident exultation of self-discovery and self-assertion was inevitably accompanied by a higher sense of purpose and moral obligation which identified itself absolutely with the aesthetic sentiment. Philosophy sharply dissociated now from religion, was reaching a point where it merged into art, into the direct, intuitive substance of art. The problem of knowledge could not be raised, nor metaphysical inquiry conducted, outside this integrality and totality of consciousness, into which in fact they resolved themselves. In the realization of this integrality and plenitude, man found the justification of his being and the focal point of all his problems. The philosophical problems of humanism, that is to say, had been organized in terms of a synthetic structure which had as its vertex and its resolvent, at one time the rational lucidity of Brunelleschi, at another the pure ideality of Piero della Francesca; and even when the pathos of Donatello or the dramatic restlessness of Masaccio came to the fore, that drama and that pathos were always the expression of a proud comparison of man with himself and with the world around him. It was a drama experienced passionately and instinctively, without any thought or suspicion of a root cause in human nature, of pangs unrelated to the positive significance of the vitality and complexity of that nature.

But the synthetic and integral phase of the discovery of man was to be followed by an analytical phase of self-scrutiny and keen investigation of the surrounding world. Then came the crisis of that integrality of consciousness in which human passions and problems had been, as it were, epitomized and subordinated, and their nucleus now emerged like a tremulous flower, with open petals. The psychological vacuum of Botticelli seems to herald the aberration of this gravitational centre of consciousness, leaving it free to oscillate from emotion to emotion, from mood to mood; while the flux of light and shade that subtly but thoroughly saturates the space of Leonardo, Botticelli's fellow pupil in Verrocchio's studio, already records the erratic departures of a thinking, seeking mind. With Botticelli, who marks the break with the original humanistic ideal, things drew to a crisis, endured with anguish; with Leonardo, who took stock of the new problems in a speculative frame of mind, that crisis was already on the way to being resolved. One brings the fifteenth century to a close, the other opens the sixteenth.

Although he follows up and consummates a certain empirical trend of Quattrocento philosophy, Leonardo is actually the first to fix and specify the new exigency of man, his demand for knowledge outside his own limits of action, and to state that exigency in terms of intellectual research and inquiry. Even though the metaphysical problem is never explicit in Leonardo, its latent, rankling presence declares itself in that sense of cosmic mystery which pervades all his art—like the sense of an echo in the infinite, an unattainable goal, that accompanies the active prosecution of his researches. But these researches undoubtedly rest on a scientific basis, they hinge on an analysis of cognitive data. In him the artist and the scientist are inseparable, not because he subscribed to the humanist postulate that art is science and knowledge in one, but because he pushed back the frontiers of art into the realm of science and embodied the problems of science in the expressive sphere of art. Whether it serves the purpose of scientific documentation or that of artistic creation, there is no change in either the values or the character of his drawing. In both cases, his is a line that probes and investigates, that delves into things acutely and indefatigably. So subtle and searching is his line that it dissolves into atmosphere, into *sfumato*, and while recording the various gradations and possibilities of knowledge, it elicits (or rather translates into cognitive terms) the limit of the mysterious and ineffable, beyond which human knowledge cannot go.

This thirst for knowledge also conditions Leonardo's attitude towards the world of feelings. Leonardo cannot be said to participate directly and subjectively in human feelings and passions, rather he objectivizes and investigates them, he seeks to take their measure. He observes their contrasts and variety, and—just as he did with bodies—studies their anatomy. He traces their transitions and gradations—in other words, he pries into human psychology, for what is psychology but a knowledge of the workings of the mind, in their infinite scale of shadings? His style, interwoven as it is with subtle passages of light and linework, is eminently suited to recording the ebb and flow of human feelings and to analysing the whole range of their subtleties.

Leonardo is known to have paid two visits to Rome, the first in 1492, the second from 1513 to 1516, when he had contacts with Leo X. The *St Jerome* by Leonardo now in the Pinacoteca Vaticana was discovered in 1820 in the shop of a Roman bric-a-brac dealer, and its provenance remains a mystery. It is, however, an early work, preceding his first visit to Rome by some years. On the strength of its affinities with the *Adoration of the Magi* in the Uffizi, it can be assigned to about 1482, shortly before he left Florence for Milan, a period in which his art had not yet reached its full maturity. Like the Uffizi painting, the *St Jerome* was left (perhaps deliberately) in the state of an unfinished sketch whose monochrome patterning effectively lays bare the essence of Leonardo's design and chiaroscuro. The devout attitude of the saint springs from the artist's interest in the psychology of his subject and from a deliberate accentuation of the mood which he set out to analyse. And though here perhaps he presses his purpose too far, the work is nevertheless indicative of that introspective line of research which culminated, with unprecedented skill and subtlety of handling, in the famous *Last Supper* (1495-1497) in Santa Maria delle Grazie, Milan.

While Leonardo was finishing the *Last Supper* in Milan, the young Michelangelo was leaving Florence for Rome where, in 1497, he was commissioned by the French cardinal Jean Bilhères de Lagraulas to carve a *Pietà*, which he completed in 1499. Set up first in Old St Peter's, in the so-called Chapel of the King of France, the work was later reinstalled in the new basilica, where it can still be seen today. Following a northern iconographic type, Michelangelo has represented the Virgin holding the body of the dead Christ in her lap. This work stands somewhat apart from the rest of the artist's output. Hitherto, in his youthful period, he had produced works which fall much more closely into line with those of his maturity, such as we shall have occasion to examine in the Sistine frescoes. This *Pietà* is Michelangelo's most "finished" piece of sculpture. In the precision of its modelling, the scrupulous rendering of the surfaces and the harmonious composition, it is far removed indeed from the usual tension and intrinsic dialectics of his greatest works. If on the one hand this is the result of deliberate virtuosity, on the other the influence of Leonardo undoubtedly had something to do with it. It has been pointed out by Charles de Tolnay that, while the intricate articulation of the drapery still recalls Jacopo della Quercia, one of the ideal masters of Michelangelo, the clear-cut rhythmical structure and the precision of the design hark back directly to Florence. Tolnay has in fact surmised that Michelangelo may have seen a drawing or print of Leonardo's *Last Supper*, as would seem to be evidenced by "the delicate features and contemplative expression of the Virgin, her gesture of resignation, the diagonal band that crosses her breast, the face of Christ with its sharp features and his brow triangularly framed by the hair."

On the whole, what seems to me to confirm the hypothesis of Leonardo's influence is the analytical, psychological element here. In treating a theme like that of the Mater Dolorosa in a psychological key, Michelangelo could not avoid lapsing into a form of pietism; a pietism which, however, he strove to lift to a pinnacle of spirituality through the nobility of the presentation. That spirituality is in a sense an indirect result, the fruit of intellectual intervention—a means, almost, of mentally atoning for a point of departure too far removed from real feeling and emotion. In making this effort, it was only natural that he should call above all on those extraordinary powers of virtuosity which he alone possessed—a virtuosity which, moreover, remains inseparable from his genuine and exceptional resources of plastic invention. The way in which the limp body of Christ cleaves to the flowing draperies of the Virgin; the development of this figure as a long, majestic silhouette, broad and sloping as a mountain; the slant of the faces, the suspension of the gestures, the rich variety of modulations and correspondences gently introduced into the harmony of the general outline—these are the inspired innovations of genius. This work marks a turning point and ushers in the sixteenth century, even though it contains in embryo the most fateful propensities of the art to come, foreshadowing its more negative features and indeed planting the seeds of academicism. Present in fact, in this *Pietà*, are the basic conditions of academic art: emotive aloofness from the theme and its sublimation in the virtuoso handling of form. With Michelangelo, however, the inner motivation that brought about these conditions, and the exigency that determined them, have conscious, historically positive sources; they have nothing in common with the gratuitousness of that aesthetic doctrine which later went by the name of academicism.

Here in fact, if Michelangelo avoids a direct emotional rendering, the reason is that he has grasped the meaning of the revolution brought about by Leonardo. For the unrestrained emotional and intellectual expansion of early Humanism, when that expansion reached the point where it conflicted with the limits and the compromises of the effective historical situation, Leonardo had substituted, as we have seen, a problematic introversion; from synthesis he had descended to analysis. Now, by way of experiment, Michelangelo took up the analytical, problematical position of Leonardo. He did not adopt it whole-heartedly, for his aims were not the same, but he made use of it provisionally as a kind of foothold enabling him to make his way forward. We have already commented on the metaphysical undertones of Leonardo's art, which conjure up a halo of cosmic mystery round the centre of his interests, which are directly concerned with the acquisition of empirical knowledge. Michelangelo, on the contrary, went in pursuit of ethical and metaphysical knowledge, and the problems this involved are those with which he dealt in the ceiling of the Sistine Chapel. From Leonardo, then, he inherited a consciousness of the new problems being raised, but pursued different aims in his attempts to solve them. While Leonardo was untouched by the tragedy and anguish of the crisis brought on by Savonarola, which so profoundly affected Botticelli and Signorelli, Michelangelo always bore the marks of that anguish, even though he sought to transmute it in an ideal tension, in a tormented concentration of thought. His soul-searchings found their resolvent in their own inexhaustible tension.

This ideal aspiration is clearly foreshadowed in the *Pietà* in St Peter's. The psychological data do not, as in the case of Leonardo, resolve themselves in a subtle self-complacency, but tend to be embodied in a moral reserve, sublimated in a noble

MICHELANGELO (1475-1564): PIETÀ, 1497-1499. CHAPEL OF THE PIETÀ, ST PETER'S.

bearing and attitude. Michelangelo felt that an ideal synthesis, direct and immediate, in which thought and feeling, passion and abstraction meet and almost merge, while it had been within reach of artists in the early phase of Humanism, was now no longer achievable. A peak of spirituality and ideality, however, could still be attained by degrees, by ascent and catharsis, through contrasting values and a hierarchical designation of them. In the *Pietà* the psychological data of suffering are thus made to convey a moral precept: through suffering man attains to sublimity. In this sense the *Pietà* is already broadly indicative of Michelangelo's spiritual travail and his yearning for catharsis. In the *Pietà* the Cinquecento is already heralded as the century of contrasts and dialectics, in contradistinction to the Quattrocento, which had been the century of syntheses.

Leonardo was in Rome in 1492, the year in which Alexander VI was elected pope. Michelangelo's first visit to Rome also took place during the pontificate of Alexander, but by 1501 he was back in Florence. In 1503, after the brief reign of Pius III, Giuliano della Rovere, nephew of Sixtus IV, was raised to the pontifical throne and took the name of Julius II. He continued the temporal policy of his predecessor, and he even more definitely cuts the figure of an Italian "prince" wholly engrossed in questions of State. His particular merit, however, was to repudiate the system of nepotism that had so much disgraced the ambiguous figure of Alexander VI and he energetically applied himself to consolidating and extending the papal dominions. This policy went a long way towards restoring the power and prestige of the Church—chiefly on the political plane, however.

Already under Alexander VI the conflict between religion and art, between Christianity and Humanism, had been resolved in a sphere of purely aesthetic interests. Any ideological or moral attitude could be justified in the name of art. This state of affairs remained unchanged under Julius II, except that the latter proved to be much more open-minded and generous than his predecessor, who had lowered art to the level of a pleasant pastime, an instrument of personal enjoyment. The ambitious schemes that actuated Julius II in his temporal policy found their counterpart in the art projects he so enthusiastically patronized. In determining to destroy the old basilica of St Peter's, the symbol and embodiment of a Christian tradition of a thousand years' standing, and to erect in its place a new temple designed on classical lines, he unhesitatingly set aside devotional and religious considerations, yielding to the love of art and cultural progress, and to a craving for magnificence whose object, however, was to enhance the prestige and power of the Papal State. He thereby created the necessary conditions for an artistic flowering such as few ages in the history of the world can rival. The Vatican thus became the capital of the Renaissance.

Underlying these achievements, there were naturally other conditions beyond the control of Julius II and implicit in the historical trend of art and thought. The fact that humanist culture, as it matured, had given rise to a whole movement of intellectual speculation, that synthetic assertion had given way to a spirit of free inquiry and investigation, that the question of "how" had been eclipsed by the question of "why and wherefore"—this fact had led to a new and fruitful junction with ancient thought: not only with the aesthetic and formal ideals of classicism, and the hedonism of pagan antiquity which had so much appealed to Quattrocento humanism, but also with the central nucleus of ancient philosophy, the metaphysical doctrines of Plato and Aristotle. That the Church should now accept, if not the guidance, anyhow the high patronage of the new culture was only natural, for on this plane aesthetic and religious interests could interact and interpenetrate. A true and intimate fusion could thus be effected between classicism and the religious conscience of Christianity, provided that religion was also considered as a philosophical problem. Michelangelo was keenly alive to this convergence of religious and philosophical interests and embodied them in his own grandiose ideology. Raphael did not react to this new climate of thought with the same intensity and whole-heartedness, and instead of attempting an effective, thorough-going fusion of these ideals, he toyed with the possibility of juxtaposing them. When in the Stanza della Segnatura he confronts the fresco of the *Disputa*, symbolizing supernatural Truth and theology, with the fresco of the *School of Athens*, symbolizing philosophy, he seems to be taking his stand midway between them, like an ecstatic spectator who, from the possibility of this "distension," elicits a new, ideal tranquillity of mind, a contemplative viewpoint equidistant from nature and God.

It is natural to assume that the spiritual position of Julius II was closer to the serenity and optimism of Raphael than to the sombre moodiness of Michelangelo, as indeed the confident assurance of his temporal policy seems to indicate. But the pope probably felt that it was the architect Bramante who by temperament was predisposed to enter most fully into his grandiose schemes and aspirations, to share his restless energies, his need of action and movement, and his love of such pageantry as gave scope for dramatic but not tragic expression.

Trained at Urbino, Bramante worked for many years in Lombardy. Gifted with all the qualities of an artist, he was particularly well known as an expert in static problems. Deeply versed in the methods of constructing vaults, he was in great demand for his resourcefulness in overcoming structural problems. About 1502 we find him in Rome at work on the small round temple—the Tempietto—in the cloister of San Pietro in Montorio. Bramante's growing reputation as an architect prompted Julius II, immediately after his election as pope, to call him in and entrust him with a vast building programme in the Vatican, involving the replanning and co-ordination of the various edifices erected almost haphazard from the thirteenth century on. Bramante probably first conferred with Julius in the early months of 1504, for in that same year he set to work on the project of heightening and enlarging the Loggia delle Benedizioni in St Peter's, a project soon afterward suspended when it was decided to tear down the church and build an entirely new one. Early in 1505 he was busily at work on the great courtyard of the Belvedere: the vast area, enclosed between two long galleries, was divided into three terraces, the upper one ending in an exedra. Bramante's project, which death prevented him from carrying out, was altered by successive architects and the overall effect intended has now been totally lost. There remains, however, the great exedra which, though modified in 1560 by Pirro Ligorio, who transformed it into a large niche, still gives an idea of Bramante's monumental conception and above all conveys an impression of the broad movement of the masses on which he centred his theme of an active and animated space.

Both Brunelleschi and Alberti had proposed a static space, planimetric and rational with Brunelleschi, monumental with Alberti, but part and parcel in both cases of a

PRINT OF THE TIME OF SIXTUS V (1585-1590) SHOWING THE VATICAN PALACE (LEFT) CONNECTED TO THE BELVEDERE PALACE (RIGHT) BY THE COURT OF THE BELVEDERE; IN THE BACKGROUND, THE VATICAN GARDENS WITH THE CASINO OF PIUS IV; AT THE UPPER LEFT, THE UNFINISHED DOME OF ST PETER'S.

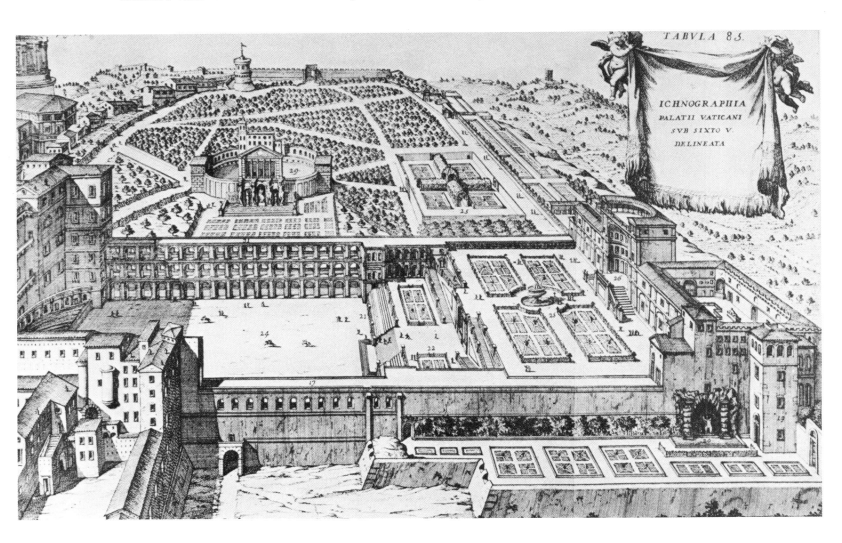

stationary, self-contained development clearly patterned or majestically encompassed by the enclosing structure. The movement of surfaces and masses peculiar to Bramante corresponds, on the contrary, to a dynamically expanding space in conflict with its own limits. The conception of Brunelleschi and Alberti reflects the moral certainty, the synthetic structure of humanist thought, of which something has already been said; whereas that of Bramante already presents the antitheses and contrasts of Renaissance thought and configures its dialectics in dynamic forms.

A parallel can be drawn in certain respects between Bramante and Leonardo, and it has already been observed that Leonardo's painting may well have supplied Bramante with subtle intimations as to the possibilities of chiaroscuro and light. But on the formal plane the comparison cannot logically be pressed any further. It does, however, repay deeper study from a point of view that we have examined before, for the correspondence between the two artists appears most strikingly in the interest Bramante showed in structure. Just as Leonardo examines and investigates anatomy, so Bramante probes thoroughly into the structure of his edifices. Not only was he the greatest architectural designer of his time and the ablest structural engineer, but his interest in these matters declares itself in the very style of his constructions, which always stress the structural elements and disclose their dynamic interaction. It was in the Gothic period that architectonic expression coincided most closely with structural content. And Bramante's study of classical architecture, from which he learned some valuable pointers regarding the statical, mathematical procedures followed in the construction of vaults, went hand in hand with a study of Gothic architecture. Formally, the fusion of Gothic and classic methods is noticeable in the increased tension vivifying the majestic build-up of volumes and in the rhythmic chiaroscuro animating them. Gothic suggested to Bramante those dramatic effects in which he

The two long wings on either side of the Court of the Belvedere were designed by Bramante to join the Belvedere Palace (right), which originally stood alone on a hill, to the lower-lying group of ancient palaces round St Peter's (left). The difference of level was compensated for by a system of stairways. At each end of the court stood an exedra. The one at the lower end was provided with steps and served as a theatre. The exedra at the upper end, crowning the terraced gardens, was transformed in 1560, by Pirro Ligorio, into a large niche—the "Nicchione"—in the form of an apse; the niche was probably designed, however, by Michelangelo, who had previously modified the stairway leading up to it. The print illustrated here shows the Court of the Belvedere after the changes made by Pirro Ligorio, but before it had been bisected by the Braccio Nuovo, or New Wing, erected by Pope Sixtus V to house the Vatican Library. In front of the niche (to the right), at the top of the double flight of stairs designed by Michelangelo, now stands the huge "Pigna," or pine-cone, a Roman bronze probably belonging originally to a fountain. In the Middle Ages the Pigna stood in the atrium of Old St Peter's, where Dante saw it (he mentions it in the *Divine Comedy*); it was moved to its present site in 1618 after the demolition of the old basilica. On each side of the Pigna is a bronze peacock from the Mausoleum of Hadrian. Within the niche is the great base of the Column of Antoninus Pius, discovered in 1703.

THE "PIGNA," OR PINE-CONE, IN THE COURT OF THE BELVEDERE. ANCIENT ROMAN BRONZE.

BRAMANTE (1444-1514) AND PIRRO LIGORIO (C. 1500-1583): THE "NICCHIONE," OR LARGE NICHE, IN THE COURT OF THE BELVEDERE.

could best embody his structural aims, which lay in giving expression to those contrasts and compounds of forces which determine the statics of the edifice. Classicism, and the visions of Piero della Francesca and Leon Battista Alberti, opened his eyes to the monumental sense of space and masses. But at the same time Bramante reacted against both the mystical abstractions of Gothic and the intellectual abstractions of Piero and Alberti. The structure, as Bramante saw it, was the soul of the building, and he made a point of focusing attention on it. The soul of a Gothic edifice is identical with that of the religious community for which it ministers; it is a collective, transcendental soul. Bramante, on the contrary, defines it in an individual sense; he seems to be seeking it out with much the same psychological interest that we noted in Leonardo. Architecture, in other words, becomes an individual organism, almost a personage, and one with a living soul.

The winding stairs in the Belvedere, the only monument still intact testifying to Bramante's activity in the Vatican, illustrate this aspect of his vision particularly well. Built in the relatively narrow space of a tower, the staircase rises with so strong an impetus that one no longer notices these limits. What we have here, however, is not the soaring thrust into the infinite of Gothic architecture, but the impatience of any limits peculiar to an expanding organism. To emphasize the spiralling impetus of the staircase, Bramante also resorts to devices of perspective, like the progressive tapering of the columns from floor to floor. Previously, in the church of San Satiro in Milan, he had gone even further, creating an apse whose spatial depth is wholly illusory, being merely an effect of perspective.

For Bramante, then, perspective is no longer what it was for Brunelleschi, an exclusively rational idea, a way of ordering and arranging space; it is no longer an end in itself, ideally established, but only a means of achieving an effect. Architecture thus assimilates possibilities peculiar to painting, and it was natural for it to do so in the ambit of a pictorial vision of architecture, like that of Bramante, who relies on emphatic chiaroscuro effects.

This space in process of expansion, criss-crossed with light and shade, bursts the mental limits of Quattrocento abstraction and brings architecture to life like an independent, individual organism. True, it is still the expression of an "idea," but it brings that idea into dialectical relation with the world of phenomena, i.e. with nature. Just as Leonardo's thirst for knowledge furthered his purpose of infringing man's egocentric isolation to embrace the surrounding reality and establish a new, more receptive attitude towards nature, so the structuralism and organic animation of Bramante's architecture imply a new outlook on the natural world. The individual characterization of his buildings, as already noted, virtually amounts to a psychological personification or, more precisely, a naturalization of the motif, whereby architecture, from its passive function of enduring and containing the actions of man that take place

BRAMANTE (1444-1514): WINDING STAIRS IN THE BELVEDERE PALACE.

within it, is promoted to an active and personal function that stimulates and indeed almost emulates the action of man. In the winding stairs of the Belvedere, the ascending movement is interpreted and actively shared by the architectonic elements: the unbroken ribbon of the parapet that reaches its climax at the top, and the sequence of columns superimposed with an accelerated rhythm, as if swept up by the spiral. Possibly Bernini had certain features of this work in mind when he conceived the main staircase, the Scala Regia, whose columns resting on the steps are admittedly personifications, directly alluding to human figures mounting the staircase.

To be sure, Bramante's naturalism has nothing in common with Baroque and is always balanced with a mental, an abstract element. What Bramante actually does, as we have said, is to bring the Quattrocento "idea" into dialectical relation with the world of phenomena. It is of course man who acts as an intermediary between the two spheres. And he acts as an intermediary in two ways: by reconciling them within himself, in other words by experiencing them both with equal ease and feeling himself equidistant from them, in a contemplative attitude, like that of Raphael; or else by observing the contrast between them and speculating on their dialectical relationship, in a tormented, controversial attitude, like that of Michelangelo. Bramante may be said not only to share both of these attitudes, but to prepare the way for them. For while on the one hand he puts the accent on the spectacular side of his new dialectical vision and interprets this meeting of forces with an almost exultant, instinctive and "natural" participation in them, on the other he seems to point out a metaphorical hierarchy of values in conflict, ranging from shadow to light, from bottom to top, from matter to mind.

The greatest undertaking assigned to Bramante in his work at the Vatican was the reconstruction of St Peter's. At the origin of this undertaking was another project, that of the great tomb of Julius II which, in March 1505, the pope himself commissioned Michelangelo to design and build. What the artist proposed was a mausoleum of colossal size adorned with forty statues disposed on three levels. Michelangelo set off at once for Carrara to pick out the finest marbles available, but during his absence the problem arose of finding a suitable location for so mighty a monument. There was no room in Old St Peter's, which was already showing alarming signs of decay in the time of Nicholas V (who had engaged Bernardo Rossellino to design a new basilica, but the project had been carried no further than the renovation of part of the apse). To house the pope's tomb it would have been necessary to finish the spacious tribune begun by Nicholas V, which meant that the Constantinian choir would have to be totally demolished. Then, however, arose the problem of joining this new building unit with the nave of the old basilica. For this Julius II called in Fra Giocondo, Giuliano da Sangallo and Bramante, but finally, in October 1505, he determined to tear down the old church and raise a new and greater one in its place. Bramante was appointed chief architect.

MICHELANGELO (1475-1564): GOD DIVIDING THE LIGHT FROM THE DARKNESS.
FRESCO ON THE SISTINE CEILING, 1508-1511.

His initial design (later modified by Bramante himself, though no record of his final design now remains) was for a basilica on the plan of a Greek cross, made to form a square by the erection of a tower at each of the four corners, with a vast dome in the centre resting on a drum with windows and four small domes on the sides. The four arms of the cross were to end in projecting, semicircular apses. "The interior of the basilica was characterized by three elements, developed like the themes of a fugue: wide spaces with curving walls, articulated and pierced, and domes; pillars which, owing to the large niches hollowed out of them, appear narrow, tall and powerful; and seven sources of light pouring down from above" (O. H. Förster).

THE SISTINE CHAPEL, LOOKING TOWARDS THE MAIN ENTRANCE.

THE SISTINE CHAPEL, LOOKING TOWARDS THE ALTAR, WITH MICHELANGELO'S "LAST JUDGEMENT" ON THE BACK WALL.

On the 18th of April 1506 the pope laid the foundation stone; by the time he died (in 1513) the four immense piers of the dome had been completed, together with the arches that spring from them. In 1514 Bramante died.

Increasingly absorbed in the work undertaken with Bramante, Julius II was compelled to give up the idea of the tomb and accordingly ordered Michelangelo to suspend the work for the time being. Enraged at the pope's decision, Michelangelo suddenly left Rome for Florence on the 17th of April 1506, just as the rebuilding of St Peter's was about to begin. But after a time the pope and the artist were reconciled and Michelangelo executed a huge statue of Julius II for the façade of San Petronio at Bologna; it was unveiled in February 1508. In May of the same year the pope called him in again and charged him with a gigantic task: to fresco the ceiling of the Sistine Chapel, which the Quattrocento artists had contented themselves with painting in blue and gold, simulating the night sky. According to Condivi and Vasari, it was Bramante who suggested the name of Michelangelo, with the spiteful intention of saddling him with a task beyond his powers, for up to that time he had worked chiefly as a sculptor and had done very little painting. But this is almost certainly a legend. Though the two artists were never on very good terms, there is no reason to suppose that either had anything but esteem for the other's work. Indeed Michelangelo's opinion of Bramante is on record. "It cannot be denied," he wrote in 1555, "that Bramante was as capable an architect as any that has ever been from the ancients up to now. He laid the foundation stone of St Peter's, not in any disorder, but clearly, frankly and luminously."

The architectonic conception of the great ceiling frescoes in the Sistine Chapel, which Michelangelo completed in October 1512, reveals several features which seem to be connected with the vision of Bramante as outlined above: the reversibility and integrability between architecture and painting; the personification of the architecture; and the dialectical contrast of forces taken as a hierarchical metaphor of moral and ideal values.

Michelangelo's first concern was to give an architectonic organization to the great surface to be frescoed, by working out in pictorial terms a framework which recast and reinterpreted the actual structure of the vault—a shallow barrel vault flanked by a series of concave triangles opening out into the lunettes above the windows. It was only as an afterthought that he decided to extend the fresco into the triangles and lunettes. The very first designs, however, show him intent on conveying the inherent tensions of the vault and taking its actual curvature into account.

"In the final execution," writes Tolnay, "Michelangelo was inspired by the real shape and the mass of the vault, in contrast with his predecessors who all sought to disguise the real form and the material weight of the vaults which they covered with their frescoes, masking the real construction either under a system of cornices or by means of illusionist paintings in *trompe-l'œil*. Michelangelo accepted the curved surface of the ceiling as it offered itself, and in it evoked an architectonic framework and a world of gigantic figures which personify the vital energies potentially present in the ceiling itself. He translated the material weight of the vault by the volume of his figures and by the *rilievo* of the painted architecture, expressing symbolically the lateral expansion inherent in the vault itself, with broad and elastic transversal arches whose tension is personified by the putti-caryatids which take the place of capitals in the pilasters. The force of cohesion counteracting the lateral expansion is expressed by a powerfully moulded cornice which runs round the bays, following the plastic projection of the pilasters and joining up the entire system. Lastly, in the large seated figures of Prophets and Sibyls, Michelangelo found the artistic symbols which explain the arched shape of the whole vault; their weight seems to pull down the gigantic architectural structure on either side."

Bramante, by introducing illusionist perspective into architecture, had integrated the qualitative and atmospheric possibilities of painting into a quantitative space. Now, in a certain sense, Michelangelo performed the reverse operation. He renounced the illusionist effects of pictorial perspective to make it cleave rather to the actual spatial measure of the architectonic structure which he intended to represent, and thereby integrated the concreteness of the architecture into the painting. The two operations, with their margin of interchangeability, meet in the hypothesis of a new equivalence between architecture and painting.

Bramante moreover, as we have seen, had conceived his constructions as individual, autonomous organisms, tantamount to personages endowed with a soul of their own, thereby aiming at a psychological personification of the architectonic theme. Michelangelo carried this architectural process of personification several stages further, even going so far as to symbolize the structural components, the thrusts and counter-thrusts, with human figures in movement, thus harking back to medieval and in particular to Gothic precedents, without however actually undergoing their direct influence. Michelangelo's point of departure was the new interest shown by Bramante in structure and in the active and symbolic significance to be attributed to the contrast of the forces embodied in that structure. We shall see presently how the personification of structural themes is directly connected, in the Sistine ceiling, with the Bramantesque principle of structure taken as the "soul" of the architectonic body.

Tolnay has observed that, owing to the gravity and plenitude of the forms, the vaulted ceiling brings to mind the majesty of Roman architecture, while by virtue of the dynamism generated by the transversal arches, which appears in open contrast with the tectonics of the classical style, it partakes of the nervous energy of Gothic architecture. Now these two components, one static (and Roman), the other dynamic

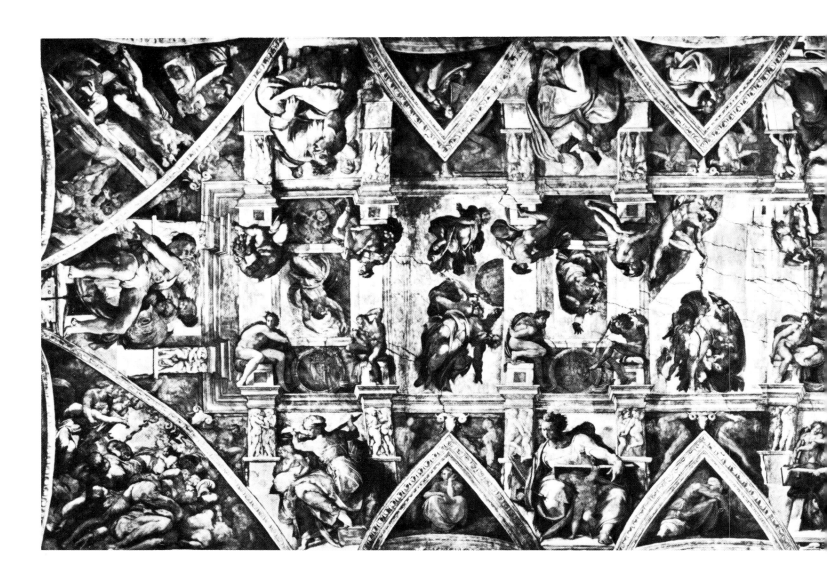

(and Gothic), are the very same as those to be found in Bramante's architecture. And in fact the reference to Bramante can probably be defined even more explicitly, for these were the very years in which he was engaged in erecting the new basilica of St Peter's. When we consider the scope of this great undertaking and the paramount importance it had assumed in all men's eyes at that time, then we need not be surprised that Michelangelo, at work in the Vatican on the Sistine ceiling, should have made an explicit reference to it, as did Raphael too in his contemporary frescoes in the Stanza della Segnatura.

Across the curving surface of his great ceiling fresco Michelangelo painted an architectonic framework consisting of five simulated arches, springing from the actual

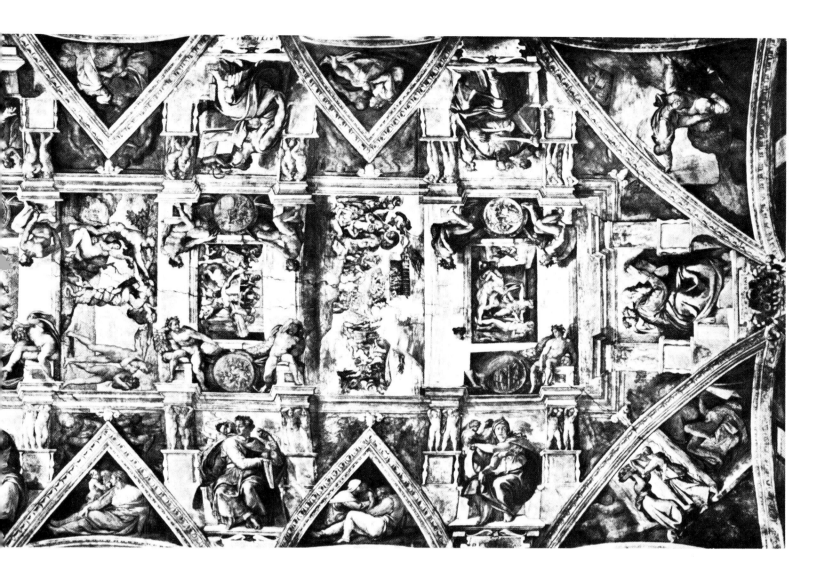

WITH MICHELANGELO'S FRESCOES, 1508-1511.

pilasters which, along the side walls of the chapel, alternate with the windows. From each of these pilasters, then, springs a mighty (simulated) arch which, as it rises overhead, spreads out and divides into two simulated pilasters. The main figures on either side—of Prophets, Sibyls and nude youths—are seated with their backs to these arches, suggesting their weight and their supporting function (within the arches are the five minor panels representing episodes from Genesis and the story of Noah). The simulated arches seem to project outward with respect to the ceiling spaces between them corresponding to the windows and concave triangles; these broad structural intervals, forming supported (and not supporting) members, are thus relieved of any weight (and in these broader spaces, free of any other figures, are the four major panels representing episodes from Genesis and the story of Noah).

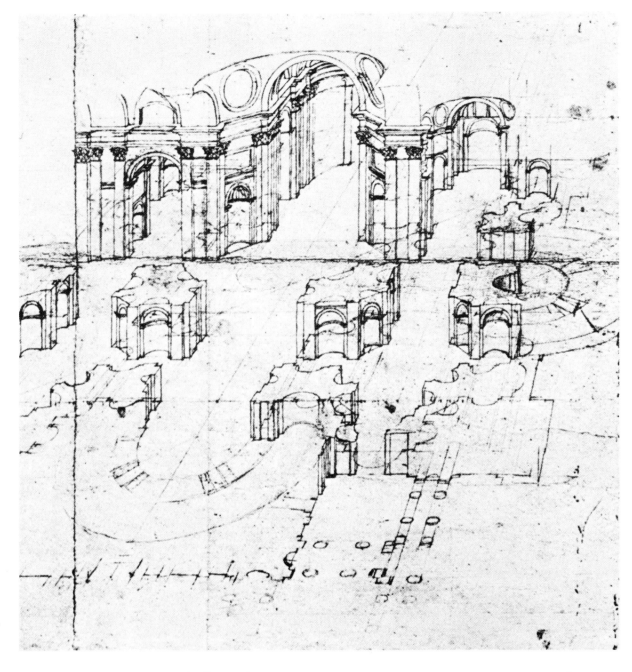

BALDASSARE PERUZZI (1481-1537): PERSPECTIVE DRAWING OF A PROJECT FOR ST PETER'S.

This layout cannot have been very far removed from the structural arrangement which Bramante had devised for the vault and wings of the new St Peter's, with large, projecting, transversal arches. In a drawing by Peruzzi based on Bramante's designs, the same concave triangles that we find in the Sistine Chapel appear to be inserted between the arches; the triangles formed part of the effective, pre-existing physiognomy of the vault, to which Michelangelo adhered, but it may now have been Peruzzi who in turn was influenced by the solution adopted by Michelangelo, while noting however its affinities with Bramante's design.

It is no reflection on Michelangelo's creative originality to assert that, in substance, the structural framework underlying the decorative conception of the Sistine ceiling owes something to Bramante; in the history of art no work is created out of nothing. Nor would this structural dynamism have interested Michelangelo if it had not stimulated his powers of invention—if, in other words, it had not been bound up (as already in Bramante, though less openly, it had been bound up) with a possibility of dialectical representation in the speculative sense, and in particular with a possible hierarchical symbology of values, on the neo-Platonic scale. Now the symbolical and philosophical purport of the fresco cycle on the Sistine ceiling has, as we shall see, been fully investigated. But it remains, perhaps, to explain, anyhow hypothetically, Michelangelo's probable intention as regards the structural framework of the ceiling which, as already noted, it would be a mistake to confine within the limits of a purely physical and optical representation of the tensions and thrusts involved.

In the sequence of episodes from Genesis and the story of Noah, five minor panels alternate with four major ones, the very considerable difference in size being due to the fact that within the simulated arches, where the nude figures are placed, the available space is much more limited. But the difference in size is also accompanied by a reduction of proportions, so much so that the disparity between the major and minor panels seems to be deliberately emphasized. Indeed it appears evident that Michelangelo resorted to this difference in format with an eye to laying particular stress on the episodes contained in the larger panels, towards which in fact, from both sides of the chapel, the lateral triangles are directed, like enormous pointers. These main compositions represent the *Creation of the Sun and Moon*, the *Creation of Man*, the *Temptation and Expulsion from the Garden of Eden*, and the *Deluge*. The other five episodes are of lesser importance; or more exactly they may be considered as leading up to the main scenes of the cycle; they are, as it were, "pre-figurations," they are the cause of which the central figurations are the effect. This explains, first, why the five "pre-figurations" are contained in the smaller panels; and, secondly, why they are located within the arches, which are weight-bearing, supporting structures, while the major episodes stand in the intermediate spaces, which are supported zones and bear no weight. And the relationship between a supporting and a supported structure is, of course, that of cause and effect; the first is the necessary condition of the second.

So beginning at the back of the chapel and moving towards the entrance (for this was the sequence followed by the Quattrocento scenes of Christ and Moses, and Michelangelo had to adopt the same orientation), the initial episode represents the *Dividing of the Light from the Darkness*; that is, the dissolution of the original chaos, which was the necessary condition for the next episode, the *Creation of the Sun and Moon*—the ordering of the cosmos. Similarly, the *Dividing of the Waters from the Land and the Creation of the Animals* is antecedent to the *Creation of Man*, of which it is the prior condition. Then comes the *Creation of Woman*, antecedent to the *Temptation and Expulsion*, of which it is clearly the cause; to emphasize the connection, note how the serpent, coiled round the Tree of Knowledge, takes the shape of a woman. The scene representing the *Creation of Woman* stands in the very centre of the ceiling, thus forming the link between the two phases of the cycle: that of the Creation on the one hand, that of man's sins and suffering on the other.

MICHELANGELO (1475-1564): GOD DIVIDING THE LIGHT FROM THE DARKNESS; THE CREATION OF THE SUN AND MOON; GOD DIVIDING THE WATERS FROM THE LAND. FRESCOES ON THE SISTINE CEILING, 1508-1511.

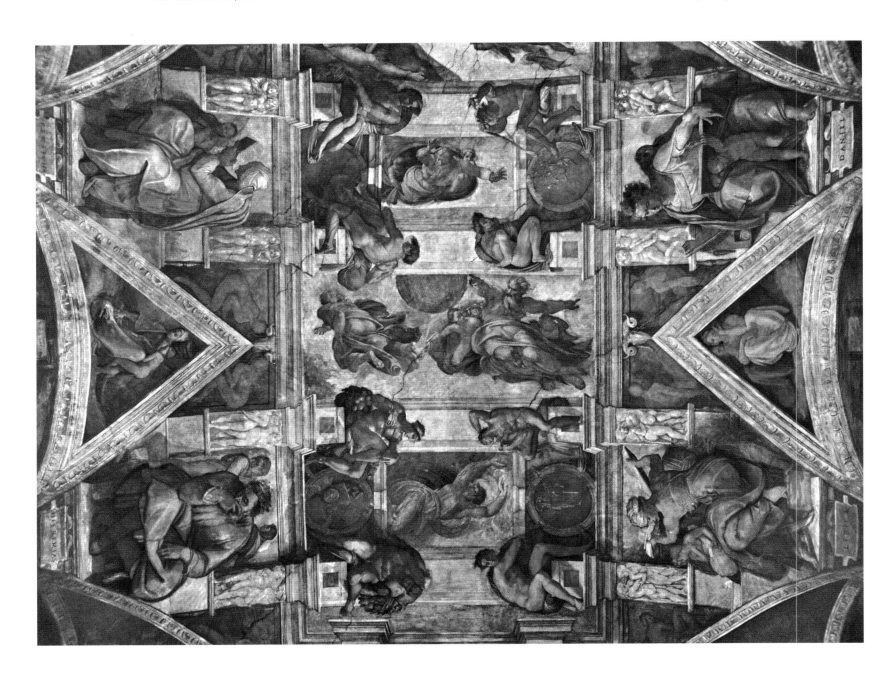

The next episode is the *Sacrifice of Noah* which, as Redig de Campos has pointed out, "should, according to the Bible, follow the *Deluge* and not precede it, as it does here; unless we regard it as an act of piety on the part of the patriarch, prior to the cataclysm, a symbol of his loyalty to God, who would then be justified in saving him in the Ark." This hypothesis, which seems to me a shrewd and convincing one, again places the smaller and the larger panel in the same relationship of cause and effect,

MICHELANGELO (1475-1564): THE SACRIFICE OF NOAH; THE DELUGE; THE DRUNKENNESS OF NOAH.
FRESCOES ON THE SISTINE CEILING, 1508-1511.

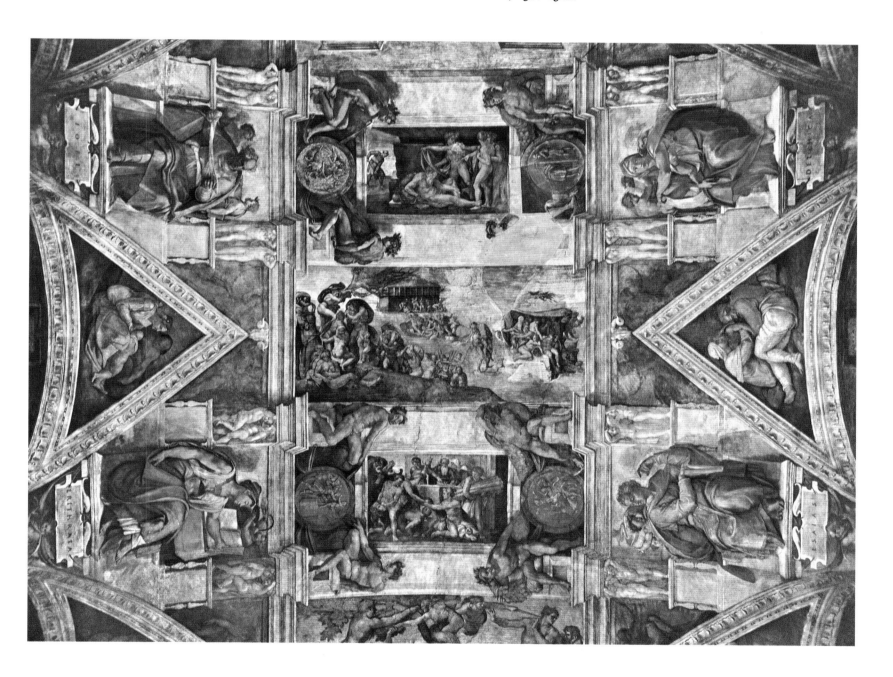

"pre-figuration" and "figuration." The cycle then comes to a close at the end of the vault with the last of the minor panels, representing the *Drunkenness of Noah*, which thus remains unassociated with any major panel. But this pessimistic conclusion of the cycle, showing man relapsing into sin, forms the connecting link—again in accordance with a cause-and-effect relationship—between Michelangelo's scenes on the ceiling and the pre-existing episodes on the side walls from the lives of Moses and Christ, "in which are evoked the promise of the redemption from evil, held out by Israel, and its fulfilment in the Passion of Christ" (De Campos).

The dialectical relationship of cause and effect, whose significance is thus brought out, according to our hypothesis, by the relation between the supporting and the supported parts of the ceiling, is well in keeping with the finalistic conception of the cycle as a whole, which sets forth a Platonic interpretation of Genesis and Original Sin. The same dualism, which lies at the origin of the world, between chaos and order, between blind necessity and rational good, recurs within man himself, composed as he is of body and soul. The soul aspires to free itself from the body, as the mind from matter and good from evil. And evil, in the Catholic vision of Michelangelo, is identified with sin.

Following the iconographic sequence of the frescoes in the opposite direction, from the *Drunkenness of Noah* to the Creation scenes (in the order, that is, in which they are seen by the visitor as he moves from the entrance towards the altar), we pass from a static phase, which reaches its apogee in the aloof and motionless figure of the Prophet Zechariah, to an increasingly dynamic phase which reaches its climax in the almost rapturous agitation of the Prophet Jonah at the far end of the ceiling. As Tolnay has written, "the spectator experiences the sensation of a progressive ascent as he advances from fresco to fresco. Identifying himself with the grandiose movement of the Supreme Being, the spectator feels himself released from the chains of earthly life and uplifted into the sphere of absolute freedom. The divine origin of the human soul makes itself manifest. This series of frescoes shows us then the return to God of the human soul imprisoned in the body, that is to say the idea of the *deificatio* or the 'return.'"

This progressive movement is accompanied, from panel to panel, by the increasing agitation of the figures of nude adolescents seated on blocks surmounting the pilasters, beneath the simulated arches of the ceiling. According to Tolnay, these nudes "are intermediate spirits between men and the divinity; since they are represented here as adolescents, without any wings, their brow encircled by the victor's headband, we should regard them as Erotes (angels reminiscent of the antique)." The present writer believes these nudes to be a personification of Eros in the strictly Platonic sense: Eros, or Love, was for Plato a divine agitation, a stimulant in man's ascent towards the eternal world of ideas. The world of sensations is the chaos to which the superior world of the intellect stands opposed. The body is the prison-house of the soul, the chain that must be burst asunder. But even in the realm of the senses, within the dark prison-house of the body, there is an aspiration towards light and order. This aspiration is Eros, and it is Eros that urges the soul to emancipate itself, Eros that gives it wings.

The two files of nudes in fact, flanking the central panels of the ceiling, are almost like wings fluttering in the air with increasing agitation as, with their progression of movement, they respond to the sense of gradual ascent which the spectator feels as he moves from the scenes of Noah to those of Genesis. And there is a further point to be made here. As we have seen in examining the architectonic organization of the ceiling, the figures personify the structural energies of the ceiling itself: the massive figures of Prophets and Sibyls plastically evoke the downward pull of gravity which anchors the ceiling to the walls, while the putti-caryatids serving as capitals express the tension exerted by the arches. What was to be the structural function of the nudes? With their plastic mass they too surely allude to the weight which the arches have to bear, but at the same time their darker volumes stand out so strongly against the light-coloured ground of the arches that they appear to be swept upward and to hover in mid-air, a movement emphasized by the vigorous freedom of their gestures. They hereby evince the upward thrust which the arches oppose to the weight of the vault. They act, that is, also in this case, as wings, and even, one might almost say, as pro-pellers. In every way then, even considered in relation to the structural organization of the ceiling, they personify Eros, i.e. the amorous longing which incites the soul to free itself from the body; and this implies that the soaring impetus of the architectural structure, in conflict with the force of gravity, in turn symbolizes the destiny of the soul in victorious conflict with the body. This is how Michelangelo harks back to Bramante's conception of structure as the "soul" of the edifice, and this is why the personification of the architectonic elements is felt to be so closely connected with that conception.

The meanings and allusions of the Sistine ceiling are many and intricate, and a full iconographic study of the figures surrounding the nine principal scenes, and of those in the triangles and lunettes besides, would lead us too far afield. Suffice it to say that the architectural framework painted by Michelangelo divides the vault into three superimposed zones. The upper zone forms the main field within the cornice enclosing the principal scenes which, as we have seen, contain the gradual revelation of the Divine. Then comes an intermediate zone occupied by the great figures of the Prophets and Sibyls, "who, while belonging to the human race, are at the same time endowed with supernatural faculties; they see with the eyes of the spirit the Divine that appears above their heads" (Tolnay). I do not think it at all unlikely that Michelangelo may have meant these figures of the Prophets and Sibyls to refer to the thinkers, philosophers, artists and scholars, who, precisely by virtue of their intellectual qualities, are closer to the Supreme Idea of God and can glimpse His light. (Here, as

MICHELANGELO (1475-1564): THE DELPHIC SIBYL, DETAIL OF THE SISTINE CEILING, 1508-1511.

MICHELANGELO (1475-1564): THE LIBYAN SIBYL, DETAIL OF THE SISTINE CEILING, 1508-1511.

Redig de Campos has observed, "the fundamental theme is still man, but the man of thought.") In this case their absorption in the books and scrolls they are holding, their rapt and wavering attitudes (note the figure of Isaiah, which Raphael took over in the *School of Athens* to represent Michelangelo himself in the guise of the pessimistic philosopher Heraclitus), and their restless tossing between the books themselves and the attraction of the celestial vision above, pointed out to them by the genii at their sides—all this may well allude to that alternative between revealed Truth and natural Truth (or philosophy) which was to be the theme, treated less dramatically but more explicitly and conciliatingly, of Raphael's contemporary frescoes in the Stanza della Segnatura. But all too often philosophical knowledge, or the knowledge of rational truth, stands in the way of Supreme Truth, it thwarts or retards the liberation of the soul. And this would explain then, in connection with the symbolism of the ceiling expressing the soul's ascension, why the figures of the Prophets and Sibyls are never assigned the plastic function of anchoring the vault and braking its upward impetus. This fact may be taken as the symptom of Michelangelo's early, pessimistic inclination towards philosophy, an inclination strengthened by his growing obsession with sin and the religious anxieties of his old age.

Finally, there is a third and lower zone, that of the triangles and lunettes, containing figurations of the "ancestors of Christ"—simple mortals seen in the drab surroundings of daily life, unsolaced by the light of revelation, just as the genii of this zone, the bronze-coloured nudes, are deprived of all light. These compositions are static, for in the absence of divine light all animation has ceased. The figures tend to be sketchlike and imperfect, obscured by dark and dreary colours. Represented in the four corner triangles of the ceiling are four scenes from the lives of David, Judith, Esther and Moses, heroes of Israel and symbols of the promised Messiah.

With this allusion to the coming of Christ, to which the figures of the Prophets and Sibyls also allude, Michelangelo emphasizes the connection between his own fresco cycle on the ceiling and the Quattrocento histories of Moses and Christ on the walls—a connection also signalized, as we have seen, by the last scene on the ceiling, the *Drunkenness of Noah*, which symbolizes man's relapse into sin, from which the price of redemption was the Passion of Christ.

There is also, I believe, an ideological filiation in a more general sense: to Plutarch, whose ideals had inspired Perugino and the artists employed by Sixtus IV, Michelangelo joins Plato. For Plutarch and Plato, as already noted, are the two thinkers of classical antiquity whose views most closely approximate to the Christian doctrine, both "by teaching and by usage," as the metropolitan John Mauropus had written as early as the eleventh century, when he besought Christ to save the souls of the two pagan philosophers from hell. The point at which the Platonic doctrine best corresponds with the Plutarchian ideal of a harmonious development of mind and body, is where Plato contemplates the possibility that the material world is but a reflection of the celestial world; where he considers Beauty to be a likeness of the divine and evokes the image of Eros as the active medium between body and soul, between tangible Beauty and eternal and ideal Beauty. Now it was on Eros that Michelangelo laid particular stress in his stupendous series of nudes, almost to the point of giving an optimistic overtone to his ideological structure, instinctively inclined though he was to pessimism—a pessimism that in fact reappears in his insistence on the theme of sin.

Actually the Eros theme forces Michelangelo to grapple with a disturbing problem: the limits between spirituality and sensuality, where Eros is concerned, are blurred and obscure; so there inevitably emerges the image of a sensual Eros which, in the Catholic eyes of Michelangelo, could only be represented as a relapse into sin. Let us consider some of these magnificent nudes. Inseparable from Michelangelo's vivid and exquisite handling of them is his delight in the sheer physical beauty of their youthful forms. So that in the very ardour which should enable the soul to free itself from the body, lies the snare of sensual desire. The free and passionate attitudes of the nudes, with their sudden and strenuous movements and their rippling muscles, do not express anguish and drama, precisely because they interpret, they embody, the contemplation of Beauty at its most exquisite moment, faintly tinged with an uneasiness verging on languor and self-surrender. But this insidious contemplation is the prelude of sin, and therefore of that anguish and drama which take on their darkest hue in the dismal vision of the "ancestors of Christ," and which find their most agitated expression, their eager need of catharsis and superabundant inspiration, in the grandiose sequence of the Genesis scenes.

Underlying the ideological and philosophical programme with which he invests it, Michelangelo's vision has its ultimate source in an unsatisfied longing; a rankling sense of restlessness which often identifies itself with an anguished consciousness of sin and aspires to purify itself by sublimating its anxieties in an intellectual tension. The mainspring of his aesthetic is catharsis—which for him meant moral redemption. Form is distended by a dynamic potential continually at the bursting point; it expands as if under the stress of a violent internal energy, but is held in check by the immovable firmness of the contours. This tension may be interpreted, in Platonic terms, as the expression of the conflict between body and soul; or, in Aristotelian terms, as the opposition between power and action, between matter and form; nor is there any real contradiction between the two interpretations. But in effect the old Platonic-Aristotelian dualism between mind and matter, the intelligible and the sensible, was re-experienced by Michelangelo as a conflict of good and evil in the sense—still historically valid—attaching to those terms in Christian ethics. Beneath the surface lay the same anguish, the same moralism that had kindled the noble aspirations of Savonarola, whose sermons Michelangelo had probably heard as a boy. Thus Michelangelo stands

THE TORSO BELVEDERE, ROMAN SCULPTURE OF THE FIRST CENTURY B.C. PIO-CLEMENTINO MUSEUM.

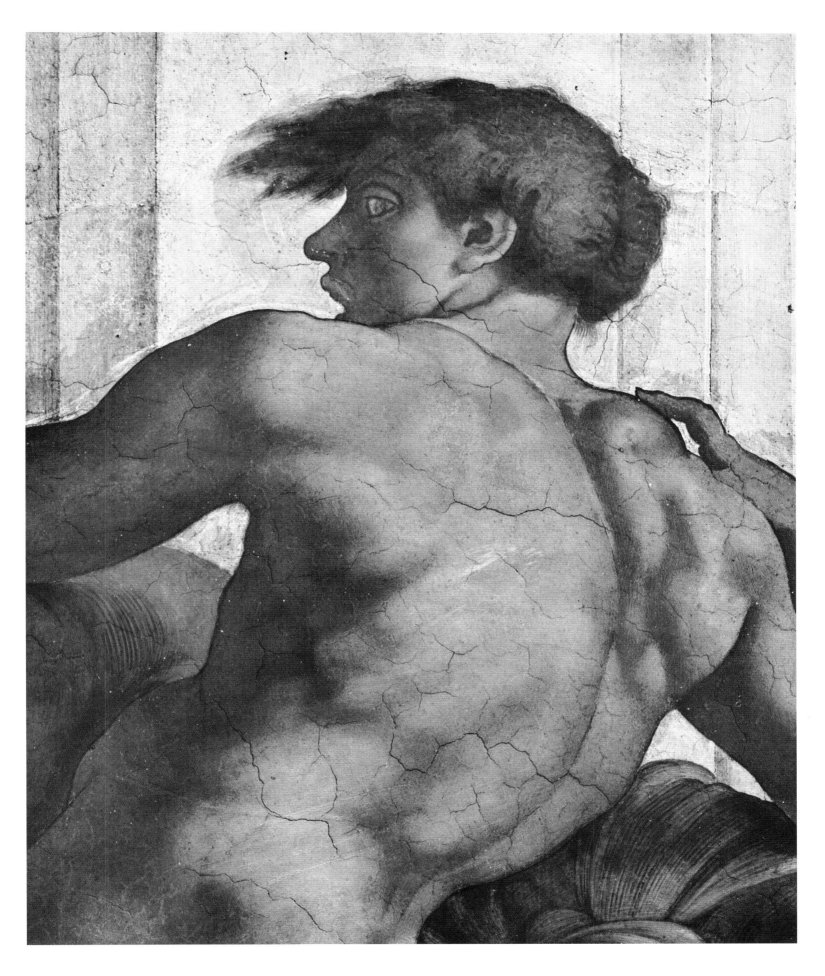

MICHELANGELO (1475-1564): NUDE YOUTH, DETAIL OF THE SISTINE CEILING, 1508-1511.

at the centre of the historical curve connecting the exhortations of Savonarola with those of the Counter-Reformation. The Renaissance as seen through Michelangelo might be likened to an arc which, eager to extend and broaden its span, stretches from one of these two poles to the other, contrasting with them both and at the same time undergoing their gravitational attraction.

In the Sistine ceiling the ultimate liberation, the breakthrough towards pure ideality, is achieved with an exuberant power and a depth of intensity which Michelangelo himself never surpassed; and achieved in more positive, more affirmative terms than elsewhere, so that his natural pessimism seems here to be counterbalanced by an optimistic element well in keeping with that ideal of equilibrium and harmony which had guided the original builders and decorators of the Sistine Chapel. Also as regards form, Michelangelo's style here rises to its highest pitch of plastic intensity, it attains its full growth, its most vigorous and positive expression, a plasticism surpassing the polished sobriety of the *Pietà* and consisting rather in the quality of a form held in tension within vibrant and powerful contours in the pure Florentine tradition. The colour is attuned to a basic chiaroscuro function, but without renouncing a wealth of contrapuntal harmonies; it is cold but fluid and luminous, like a mellow patina emphasizing the sculpturesque quality of the figures and at the same time bringing them vividly to life.

In this tremendous effort of man to transcend himself and surmount the limits, both moral and intellectual, of earthly life, the vision of Michelangelo finds full justification for its titanic proportions. Leonardo's searching investigations in pursuit of knowledge, the structuralism and dynamism of Bramante, the overwrought anxieties of Botticelli in his last phase, the dramatic tumult of Signorelli—these represent constituent elements, whether moral or formal (and often both together), of Michelangelo's vision; and to these elements were added, on the purely stylistic plane, other precedents stemming directly from the Florentine tradition. There remains, however, a further, fundamental factor which played a decisive part in shaping Michelangelo's style after his second trip to Rome, and this was his study of antique statuary, in particular of the famous *Laocoön* group discovered in 1506 during excavations on the Esquiline. This marble statue is identifiable with the one described by Pliny and carved, according to him, by Athenodorus, Agesander and Polydorus, of Rhodes. Belonging to the Hellenistic phase of Greek art, it dates almost certainly to the second century B.C. It is based on the myth of the priest Laocoön who, having warned the Trojans against the wooden horse left by the Greeks, was attacked by a serpent and killed, together with his two sons. According to the most ancient version of the story, Laocoön was not punished by Athena, who detested Troy and was determined on its downfall, but was sacrificed by Apollo in order to save part of the Trojan population. Laocoön and his sons are represented struggling desperately in the serpent's coils; the spirit accepts the sacrifice but the flesh rebels.

THE LAOCOÖN GROUP, HELLENISTIC SCULPTURE OF THE SECOND CENTURY B.C. PIO-CLEMENTINO MUSEUM.
LEFT, AS RECONSTRUCTED IN THE SIXTEENTH CENTURY; RIGHT, AS RESTORED TO ITS ORIGINAL STATE.

The *Laocoön* group was unearthed on January 14, 1506, in the ruins of the so-called Baths of Titus, in the vineyard of one Felice de' Freddi, who in the epitaph on his tomb in Santa Maria d'Aracoeli boasts of his wonderful discovery. The group was at once recognized as the one described by Pliny the Elder as the work of the Rhodian sculptors Athenodorus, Agesander and Polydorus. Pope Julius II acquired the statue and had it placed in the orange grove of the Belvedere Palace where, in niches designed by Bramante, the papal collection of ancient marbles was being gathered together. This garden of statues, opened to artists by Julius II, may be considered as forming the original nucleus of the Vatican Museums. To the *Laocoön* Julius soon added the famous *Apollo Belvedere*, the *Torso Belvedere*, the *Venus Felix*, the *Ariadne Sleeping*, the *Meleager*, and the statues personifying the Nile and the Tiber. The *Laocoön* group was restored and reassembled in the sixteenth century by G. A. da Montorsoli, who added the missing right arms to the three figures and completed the coils of the serpent round the arm of Laocoön himself. These arbitrary additions, however, disrupted the intricate, skilfully balanced rhythm of the group; the movement of the lines, meant to be broad and sweeping, while turning ceaselessly back upon itself, was deflected upward in Montorsoli's reconstruction (left) and given an unwarrantedly high point of focus. The work has recently been restored to its original state (right), the sixteenth century additions being eliminated and a newly discovered fragment of the arm being added to the central figure; though it is still incomplete, the original form and conception of the group are now clearly conveyed. The discovery of the *Laocoön* gave a new direction, and a new sense of dynamism, to the researches of Michelangelo and also of Raphael; in a more general way, the ultimate consequences of its influence appeared a century later in Baroque, which made of exuberant movement a stylistic principle.

CENTRAL FRAGMENT OF THE LAOCOÖN GROUP. PHOTOGRAPH TAKEN DURING THE RECENT RESTORATIONS.

The sublimity of the theme, which rises directly out of the expression of the work, could not but fascinate Michelangelo and the *Laocoön* became almost an idol in his eyes. It suggested to him the figurative motif, and perhaps also the idea, of his favorite theme, that of the conflict between mind and matter, between body and soul. The plastic tension of the marble group (often unjustly taxed with mannerism, whereas in fact it directly conveys the full impact of forms in movement), the writhing of the limbs and the spasmodic swelling of the muscles under the stress of strenuous effort, all suggest specific correspondences with the vision of Michelangelo.

The *Laocoön* group is composed of four larger and three smaller pieces, which were refitted together in the sixteenth century and arbitrarily integrated by Montorsoli; it was recently restored and disengaged from the parts added to the original. The photographs made during the restoration—for example the one of the great central fragment of Laocoön himself—show us the work as it must have appeared when first discovered. The marble fragment of Laocoön's figure, turning and twisting as if emerging from a struggle with time and oblivion, seems to be even more Michelangelesque, than the group as a whole; it brings to mind the broken, impeded tension of the *Captives* intended for the tomb of Julius II. Another famous fragment of antique sculpture was known to Michelangelo and much admired by him: the so-called *Torso Belvedere*, discovered in the early sixteenth century, a work signed by the Athenian sculptor Apollonius, son of Nestor, who lived in Rome toward the end of the Republic. The concentrated plasticism of this mutilated trunk (perhaps belonging to a figure of Hercules), its powerful torsion and the broad, strongly marked play of the muscles, are all so many features which, with those inspired by the *Laocoön*, reappear almost unchanged in the figures on the Sistine ceiling.

In the very years in which Michelangelo was working in the Sistine Chapel, Raphael was painting his frescoes in the Stanza della Segnatura (1508-1511). Unwilling to live in the Borgia Apartment, with its unpleasant memories of Alexander VI, Julius II decided to establish his residence in another suite of four rooms, or *stanze*, in the Vatican. The last of these rooms, the Sala di Costantino, which was to be decorated largely by Giulio Romano and Gianfrancesco Penni, formed part of the ancient palace of Nicholas III, while the other three, frescoed by Raphael, had been built by Nicholas V. These rooms had already been decorated with some frescoes by such famous artists as Piero della Francesca, Luca Signorelli, Bramantino and Bartolomeo della Gatta. When Raphael arrived in Rome toward the end of 1508, a new group of painters, among them Perugino, Peruzzi, Sodoma and Lotto, was at work in the *stanze*. But Julius II, with the same quickness of decision, the same intolerance of compromise that had prompted him to rebuild St Peter's anew from the ground up, now decided to sweep the old frescoes away and have the rooms entirely redecorated by Raphael, then the rising star among the younger generation of painters, introduced to the pope by Bramante.

Raphael set to work in the second room, later called the Stanza della Segnatura (the "signature room," where the pope heard appeals and signed pardons), but originally the library of Julius II. The subject-matter of the frescoes accordingly respects the order in which the different branches of knowledge followed each other in humanist libraries: Theology, Philosophy, Jurisprudence and Poetry, symbolic figures of which appear in the four medallions on the ceiling. Alternating with the medallions are four panels, one at each corner, on the following themes, each having some special meaning with reference to the medallion it adjoins: Adam and Eve (referring to Theology, the science of revealed Truth; for just as cause leads to effect, so the Original Sin led to the coming of Christ and thus to the Revelation); Astronomy (referring to natural or rational Truth, i.e. to Philosophy), in the allegorical guise of a female figure spinning a large globe; the Judgement of Solomon (referring to Justice and the Good); and Apollo and Marsyas (referring to Poetry and the Beautiful). The other paintings on the ceiling (decorative designs and smaller panels) are probably anterior to Raphael; according to Vasari, they are Sodoma's work. As a matter of fact the panel with Apollo and Marsyas reveals a style seemingly distinct from Raphael's, and may be the work of Peruzzi: the forms, weak and elongated, lack the springiness and vibrancy, the flickering chiaroscuro, that we find in the other panels, notably in the "Judgement of Solomon," compositionally akin to it, whose freshness of invention is vouched for by the preliminary designs in Raphael's own hand.

The frescoes on the walls refer to the same themes as the ceiling panels. On the two main walls, opposite each other, are the two great frescoes of the *Disputa del Sacramento* and the *School of Athens*, symbolizing revealed Truth (theology) and natural or rational Truth (philosophy). The "Dispute of the Sacrament," the name by which the first fresco is traditionally known, is a misnomer, arising from the erroneous interpretation of a passage in Vasari; the fresco actually represents the Church glorious and the Church militant. In the upper zone the Trinity is represented in the centre, between the Virgin and St John the Baptist, with a row of saints to right and left. In the lower zone, on either side of an altar on which the Holy Sacrament is displayed, are gathered the Doctors of the Church and the most enlightened exponents of Theology, among them Dante, Savonarola and an old man in Dominican robes who may probably be identified as Fra Angelico.

The *School of Athens* represents, beneath the mighty vaults of a stately basilica, a numerous assembly of the great philosophers of ancient Greece. In the centre is Plato (his features are those of Leonardo), engaged in discussion with Aristotle and pointing to the heavens (i.e. the world of Ideas) with the forefinger of his clenched and upraised hand; Aristotle holds out his open hand before him, between heaven and earth, with downward palm, as if opposing to Plato's soaring idealism a dialectical and organic vision of reality embracing the universal and the particular. Not all the figures have been identified, but recognizable among them are Socrates on the upper left in the

RAPHAEL (1483-1520): CEILING OF THE STANZA DELLA SEGNATURA, 1508-1511.

company of Alcibiades and Alexander dressed as a warrior; the cynic Diogenes sprawling half naked on the steps; the hedonist Epicurus crowned with vine leaves, on the lower left; and meditating in the foreground, the pessimist Heraclitus (with the features of Michelangelo); on the lower right are the geographer Ptolemy with the terrestrial globe and Zoroaster with the celestial globe. Recognizable in this same group is Euclid (portrayed as Bramante), bending with his compass over a slate, and bearing the abbreviated signature of Raphael on the hem of his tunic. On the extreme right of this group, looking out of the picture, are the figures of Raphael himself, with a black cap, and Sodoma dressed in white. It seems to me worthy of note that, while Raphael has placed Michelangelo, in a brooding, irresolute attitude, among the "thinkers," he himself, together with Bramante, stands in the group of astronomers, geometers and mathematicians; and he has sealed this choice by placing his signature (deciphered by Redig de Campos) on the figure of Euclid-Bramante.

On the two smaller walls of the Stanza della Segnatura, facing each other, are *Mount Parnassus* and the *Cardinal and Theological Virtues*, symbolizing the Beautiful and

RAPHAEL (1483-1520): PREPARATORY DRAWING FOR THE "JUDGEMENT OF SOLOMON."
ASHMOLEAN MUSEUM, OXFORD.

RAPHAEL (1483-1520): THE JUDGEMENT OF SOLOMON, 1508-1511.
DETAIL FROM THE CEILING OF THE STANZA DELLA SEGNATURA.

the Good. Beneath the fresco of the "Virtues" are two scenes forming a kind of appendix to it, one on either side of the window: *Gregory IX receiving the Decretals from St Raymond of Penafort* and *The Emperor Justinian receiving the Pandects from Trebonianus*. These two scenes allude to canon and civil law respectively, which are the juridical embodiment of the Good. The "Parnassus" fresco represents Apollo seated on the sacred mount surrounded by the Muses and a group of ancient and medieval poets, among them Homer, Sappho, Petrarch, Virgil and Dante, the latter tellingly portrayed in profile, his strong features and figure standing out sharply, in isolation, against the background sky.

Taken as a whole, the fresco sequence in the Stanza della Segnatura celebrates the three ideas of the True, the Good and the Beautiful, which according to the principles of Neo-Platonism constitute the fundamental categories of the human spirit. The parallelism with the Sistine ceiling is not only chronological; the two works have themes in common which shed light on the profound difference between their development. Common to both is the general neo-Platonic scheme. Then there is the contrast between revealed Truth and rational Truth which, according to our hypothesis, also occurs in the Sistine ceiling, through the metaphor of the Prophets. Further, the Platonic theme of the ascent to the world of ideas, which in Michelangelo assumes mystical and central accents, is probably also present, but in more abstract and peripheral guise, in Raphael. The connection between the wall frescoes, where the True, the Good and the Beautiful are exemplified, and the ceiling medallions where the same ideas are on the contrary symbolized, may allude to a transition from the concrete to the abstract, from the sensible to the intelligible. Lastly the reference to the architecture of Bramante and to the new basilica of St Peter's, which we thought to discern in the painted framework of the Sistine ceiling, reappears explicitly, in token of confirmation, in Raphael's frescoes: in the *Disputa* (which celebrates the Church glorious and the Church militant) the block of marble on the right seems to allude to the foundations of the new church, then in process of construction; in the *School of Athens*, as Adolfo Venturi has written, the new church of St Peter's "comes vividly to life in Raphael's imagination," in grandiose, Romanizing forms, typically Bramantesque, so much so that tradition has it that Bramante himself designed the architectural setting of this fresco.

In the new church of St Peter's, then, Michelangelo and Raphael saw either the image of the Church *par excellence* or the most solemn architectonic embodiment of the neo-Platonic ideology—the place, that is, where Christianity and Humanism were destined to celebrate their sublime union. But in the *School of Athens* Raphael strips Bramante's architecture of that dramatic force, that vast tissue of interplaying light and shade, which had so much appealed to Michelangelo, to interpret it rather in terms of a nobly measured, far-reaching expanse of space, sweeping overhead with serene regularity, like concentric ripples on water. The picture space stretches away like

Facing each other on the two main walls of the Stanza della Segnatura are the *Disputa*, symbolizing theology, and the *School of Athens*, symbolizing philosophy. Together these two works represent the ideal of the Italian Renaissance: the union of religion and philosophy, of Christianity and classical antiquity. The *School of Athens* shows an assembly of the great philosophers, poets and men of science of ancient Greece. The two central figures, framed in an arch and seen against the open sky, are Plato (a portrait of Leonardo da Vinci) and Aristotle, engaged in a philosophical discussion. A little to the left, in a green robe, stands Socrates, counting off his arguments on his fingers. Writing in the centre foreground, with his head on his hand, is the pessimistic philosopher Heraclitus (a portrait of Michelangelo). On the right is Bramante, portrayed as Euclid, bending over a geometrical diagram. The last two figures on the extreme right are portraits of Raphael himself, with a dark cap, looking out of the picture, and Sodoma, dressed in white. The stately building in which all these figure groups are arranged is modelled on Bramante's designs for St Peter's.

The traditional title of this fresco, the *Disputa del Sacramento*, or "Dispute on the Sacrament," is a misnomer; the real theme is the Church glorious and the Church militant. Here, writes Vasari, "the master has depicted Heaven, with Christ and the Blessed Virgin, St John the Baptist, the Apostles, the Evangelists and the Martyrs, all enthroned amid the clouds; and above them is the figure of God the Father, who sends forth His Holy Spirit over them all, but more particularly on a vast company of Saints who are celebrating Mass below, and some of whom are discoursing concerning the Host which is on the altar. Among these are the four Doctors of the Church (to wit, SS. Jerome, Augustine, Ambrose and Gregory the Great), who are surrounded by many Saints, namely St Dominic, St Francis of Assisi, St Thomas Aquinas, St Bonaventura Duns Scotus, and Nicholas of Myra. Dante, Savonarola, and all the Christian theologians are also depicted, and a vast number of portraits from life. In the air above are four cherubim who are holding open the Four Gospels; these are figures which it would not be possible for any painter to surpass, such is their grace and perfection."

a series of majestic, gently curving rings which, moving forward from a distant vanishing point, gradually grow larger as they advance towards the spectator, seeming at last to sweep him up in their embrace. The spectator stands in fact at the ideal point of convergence of spatial developments which, stemming from opposite poles, from the *Disputa* on the one hand and the *School of Athens* on the other, emerge and unite in the room itself: two worlds of ideas, religion and philosophy, become one.

The gentle and progressive rhythm of this unfolding space, together with the restful, expansive mood of this longed-for symbiosis of ideologies, which seems to reveal a definite lack of interest in the dialectics of the problems at issue and to express, rather, the aspiration towards a contemplative intermission—all this is too well in keeping with the style and the psychology of Raphael for it to be credible that the architectural setting was really designed by Bramante. Raphael may well have consulted Bramante but the conception is his own.

Michelangelo took a share, and a dramatic one, in the issues at stake. His urgent need of catharsis led him to adhere to the mystical and dialectical substance of the Platonic ideology and to seek to reconcile it with Catholic ethics, which effectively corresponded to his deepest feelings. The theologico-philosophical programme of the Sistine ceiling, its complex symbolism, forms an integral part of Michelangelo's vision, inseparable from the expressive content of that vision and, by the same token, from the organic structure of his forms. For Raphael, on the other hand, Neo-Platonism was an ideological postulate which he accepted *a priori*, a philosophical fashion, so to speak, to which he conformed, an aulic and official doctrine more attractive in its attributes than in the hard core of problems which it raised; indeed, the aulic and the official merge in the spatial conception of his frescoes. This doctrinal and symbological programme then, while in Michelangelo it gives rise to a personal meditation, in the Stanza della Segnatura undoubtedly reflects the suggestions of some of the scholars of the Roman Curia; it is like a mental superstructure, or substructure, the scaffolding of a disembodied vision directed towards an ideal world of another timbre, palpable and naturalistic. Hence the clarity of exposition, the didactic explicitness, the official-minded, faintly adulatory conformism of this programme, unquestioningly accepted.

For Raphael, always respectful of order and authority, and official interpreter of a culture, it was therefore not very difficult to do what Michelangelo, with the best will in the world, failed to do: to hark back to the neo-Plutarchian ideals of the Sistine, as interpreted by his master Perugino, and to reconcile Platonism with them, selecting from the Platonic system its most suitable and optimistic themes. In this operation Raphael acted with sincerity and conviction. He shared Perugino's ideal of harmony, and the Platonic conception of Beauty as the tangible image of the Idea accorded with his naturally contemplative turn of mind, leaning not to the transcendental but to the immanent.

MAERTEN VAN HEEMSKERCK (1498-1574): WASH DRAWING SHOWING THE INTERIOR OF ST PETER'S
ABOUT 1534. KUPFERSTICHKABINETT, BERLIN.

This drawing by the Dutch painter Maerten van Heemskerck, who spent several years in Rome (between 1532 and 1536), shows the new St Peter's in process of construction. From the great barrel vault of the new church, designed by Bramante, Raphael took inspiration for the spacious architectural setting of the *School of Athens*. In 1538 a dividing wall was built between the new part of the basilica and the Constantinian nave; the latter, with its ancient columns, is clearly visible here in the right and left foreground.

Raphael never aspired to a transcendental sphere, nor did he oppose the sensible to the intelligible or ever dwell on the conflict between mind and matter, between body and soul. He contemplated the spectacle of nature with keenly responsive senses. While Michelangelo considered the senses an obstacle to the attainment of the transcendental, which was the be-all and end-all of his ideology, Raphael took the opposite view. The empyrean world of Ideas interested him only in so far as a reflection of it is perceptible in the visible world here below. Now according to Plato we can perceive that reflection in geometric figures and mathematical relationships; the good and the beautiful reveal themselves in symmetry and proportion. Here, then, are the function and the latent symbolic meaning of perspective, which orders and harmonizes natural and tangible space without either transcending or sublimating it, but by becoming an integral part of it, an expression of its organic structure, a receptive channel giving direction and purpose to the flux of the tangible, a vessel in which it expands and pervades the walls. And here, it seems to me, is why Raphael, in the *School of Athens*, made a point of placing himself and his friend Bramante among the geometers and mathematicians, standing well apart from Michelangelo.

Already in the first half of the fifteenth century with Nicholas of Cusa (1401-1464), humanistic Platonism had given rise to a gradually maturing trend of immanence thought, a doctrine which may be summed up as follows: though unknowable, God is present in and throughout all created things, as the eternal form which gives being to their nature. This trend of thought developed into an attitude of pantheistic naturalism with Bernardino Telesio (1509-1588) and Giordano Bruno (1548-1600). Now Raphael's outlook seems to me to fit into this movement of ideas, and to have its place between the immanence doctrine of Nicholas of Cusa (a system in which, be it noted, mathematics played a key part as a stepping stone to the unattainable knowledge of God, and almost as a substitute for that knowledge) and the naturalism of Telesio who, while not renouncing traditional metaphysical reasoning, held all human knowledge to derive from the senses. Leonardo might in many respects be regarded as an exponent of the same line of thought. The difference is that Leonardo lays stress on the speculative problem of knowledge (God, admittedly unknowable, manifests himself as a mysterious presence in all things, which in themselves are knowable by way of the senses); whereas for Raphael this philosophical approach is but the historical premise, mentally unelaborated, of an artistic attitude which, to its poetic motives, joins the positive data of sensory responses and the pure mathematical intuition of God as the order and proportion immanent in nature—an attitude which tends to rise above the problems involved and stand free in self-contemplation.

Raphael, moreover, often refers back to Leonardo's *sfumato*. The naturalistic, covertly pantheistic bent of his mind also explains his transpiring predilection for the colours of the Venetians, as an open vehicle of sensibility (in the Stanza d'Eliodoro, to be sure, the role of colour is more extensive, but already in Raphael's early training there was a Giorgionesque element); and all resolves itself in a mellow chiaroscuro which, without nullifying their internal plastic autonomy, envelops figures and softens their masses. This same fluid pervades—without saturating it—the entire picture space and sensitizes the walls.

RAPHAEL (1483-1520): PORTRAIT OF DANTE, DETAIL OF THE "PARNASSUS." STANZA DELLA SEGNATURA.

RAPHAEL (1483-1520): PORTRAIT OF ARISTOTLE, DETAIL OF THE "SCHOOL OF ATHENS." STANZA DELLA SEGNATURA.

From Leonardo, Raphael also borrowed the leisurely spacing of his compositions (the *Disputa* and the *School of Athens* are good examples of this), linking the parts together with a series of psychological transitions, which he expresses largely by means of gestures; indeed the connective interplay of significant gestures in the *School of Athens* has a precedent in Leonardo's *Last Supper*. From Perugino, on the other hand, his compositions take over—and develop on broader lines—the sense of symmetry as rhythm and, even more, the criterion of a studied distribution of figure groups. Raphael places his figures in space like clay models; each position in space thus occupied answers to an internal rhythmic cadence and to a proportional relationship of the figure with other figures and with space itself.

His quest of equilibrium and naturalistic space oriented Raphael's sympathies towards the Quattrocento frescoes in the Sistine Chapel, whose schematic design, however, he meant to go beyond. And in this connection he seems now to have also taken an interest in Botticelli's frescoes, which do violence to this schematic space in an attempt to open it out to the infinite. The *Disputa* contains a distant allusion to the composition of Botticelli's *Purification of the Leper*, in the way the two files of figures descend and converge towards the centre, throwing back the vanishing point to the far distance; this type of composition is even more strikingly exemplified in the *Adoration of the Magi*, a panel which Botticelli painted almost certainly in Rome, while at work in the Sistine Chapel, and which Raphael might easily have seen.

But space in the *Disputa*, though broadly extended, is not dispersed; it has an internal order which gives it structure and binds it to an ideal centre. It resembles a cupola, or an apse, curving deeply but defined by its own curvature, and identifying itself with the bowl of the sky. That sky is full of air and atmosphere, it breathes deeply over the landscape: the ideal world and the world of nature tend to interpenetrate and balance each other.

From 1512 to 1514 Raphael was at work on the decoration of the next room, the Stanza d'Eliodoro. On one of the two main walls he painted the *Expulsion of Heliodorus from the Temple* (illustrating the incident described in the Second Book of Maccabees, and probably alluding to the energetic policy of Julius II in his struggle against the usurpers of papal territories); on the other is the *Repulsion of Attila from the Walls of Rome by Leo the Great*. On the two smaller walls he painted the *Angel delivering St Peter from Prison* and the *Miracle of Bolsena*. The presiding theme of the whole cycle seems to be the divine intervention in defence of the integrity of the Faith and the spiritual and temporal patrimony of the Church.

Less concerned here with a theologico-philosophical programme, Raphael strikes perhaps a note of greater sincerity and certainly achieves a greater degree of ease and freedom in the narrative, while drawing more abundantly on the light and colour resources of the painter's medium. The clear and mellow tones of the Stanza della Segnatura give place to a warmer, richer palette, with Venetian undertones, but articulated, in the light-and-shadow play of the compact masses, in terms of a clean-cut, well-proportioned spatial structure. These features find their most telling expression in the impeccable compositional equilibrium of the *Miracle of Bolsena*.

In the *Angel delivering St Peter from Prison*, where Raphael's fancy ranges more freely and to greater heights than ever before, the light element comes into play, in an extraordinary orchestration of themes: in the background the light of the moon

RAPHAEL (1483-1520): THE MIRACLE OF BOLSENA (CENTRAL FRAGMENT), 1512-1514.
ON THE RIGHT, PORTRAIT OF POPE JULIUS II HEARING MASS. STANZA D'ELIODORO.

RAPHAEL (1483-1520): THE ANGEL DELIVERING ST PETER FROM PRISON, PRELIMINARY DESIGN FOR THE
FRESCO IN THE STANZA D'ELIODORO. WASH DRAWING, UFFIZI, FLORENCE.

mingles with that of the dawn, while the interior of the prison, still plunged in
darkness, is revealed in the divine radiance emanating from the angel and the glow
of the torches held by the sentinels. For this invention there was a precedent, similar
in conception, in Piero della Francesca's *Dream of Constantine* at Arezzo (in which the
miracle also takes place while the protagonist is asleep); but in addition there are
stylistic reminiscences of Venetian painting (Lorenzo Lotto, be it remembered, had
worked in these very rooms). And Raphael, once again, stands mid-way between
ideal abstraction (here the reference may well be to Piero) and naturalism (which
forms the common ground between Raphael and the Venetians). The action unfolds in
a state of suspension between sleep and waking, on the edge of a dream; Raphael
succeeds in expressing to perfection the subdued and glowing rapture of his poetic
temperament, surrendering himself to the theme of the dream, in which the natural
and supernatural, the sensible and suprasensible interweave and merge in a soft and
soothing abandon.

RAPHAEL (1483-1520): THE ANGEL DELIVERING ST PETER FROM PRISON (DETAIL), 1512-1514.
STANZA D'ELIODORO.

Into the *Expulsion of Heliodorus* there enters the dynamic element—movement. This new orientation of Raphael's style is usually regarded as evidence of Michelangelo's influence; and undoubtedly the strenuously contorted forms in this scene owe something to Michelangelo. But this dynamism is also a consequence of Raphael's new interest in light, and above all of the vitality inherent in the artist's happy, expansive nature. It represents the transition from a receptive to a more explicitly participative phase in his contemplation of nature, seen as an open spectacle in movement, traversed by the flux of the tangible; and here he also links up with the spectacular and naturalistic side of Bramante's architecture, to which reference has been made. The stirring theme of the *Expulsion* actually calls for this new agitation and translates it, in this case, into an apparently dramatic inspiration which conceals the joyful, extroverted content.

A shaft of light traverses the fine series of gilded cupolas receding in perspective (creating a spectacular tension that brings to mind Bramante's winding stairway in the Belvedere) and like a whirlpool pours into the right side of the composition, where three angels are assailing the fallen robber general Heliodorus, while on the left, out of the light and out of the action, calmly looking on, sits Julius II with his attendants.

In the Middle Ages a moral distinction had been drawn between the two sides of the human figure: the right side (i.e. the left for the spectator) closed and placed under the divine protection, the other open and exposed to the power of evil. This distinction was taken over by Michelangelo in his *David*, and I believe that Raphael now reverted to this concept, applying it to the entire composition: motionless and blocked on one side, open and in movement on the other. This hypothesis is borne out, it seems to me, by a comparison with the fresco on the opposite wall, the *Repulsion of Attila by Leo the Great*: static in the zone where, as in the previous fresco, the figure of the pope appears with his retinue, safely placed under divine protection; fraught with action on the other side of the composition, where Attila and his hordes are represented— action in crescendo, expanding towards the opposite side of the scene (the right side, from the spectator's point of view).

In the figure of Leo the Great we now have a portrait not of Julius II, who died in February 1513, but of his successor Leo X, the Florentine Giovanni de' Medici, who embarked on a much less aggressive policy, seeking to steer the Church into the ways of peace. Good-natured and easy-going, an aesthete refined, generous and a little superficial, the new pope lavishly patronized the arts and encouraged public rejoicings. "It would be a picture of infinite variety, painted in a thousand colours," writes Gregorovius, "if we could describe a single year of Roman life in the time of Leo X, and call to mind the continuous series of festivities that were celebrated then, in the strangest mixture of paganism and Christianity: carnival masquerades, pageants of ancient mythology, episodes of Roman history represented with magnificent sets; in addition

RAPHAEL (1483-1520): THE EXPULSION OF HELIODORUS FROM THE TEMPLE, 1512-1514.
STANZA D'ELIODORO.

processions and splendid church feasts and representations of the Passion in the Colosseum, and classical declamations in the Campidoglio, and further festivals and discourses on the anniversary of the founding of Rome; and every day cavalcades of cardinals, and ceremonies marking the arrival of ambassadors and princes, with retinues so numerous as to seem like armies."

The pessimism of Michelangelo was out of keeping with this atmosphere. So was the intense introspection of Leonardo, who came to Rome in 1513 and, unable to find steady employment under the new pope, left again in 1516. Raphael, meanwhile, triumphed and held the field. On Bramante's death in 1514 he was appointed chief architect of the Vatican Palace and St Peter's and prefect of antiquities in Rome.

Leaving behind him for good the problems of Platonism, Raphael turned now towards the faintly pantheistic, almost animistic, but serenely "natural" vision of the Loggie,

149

the open galleries round the Court of St Damasus in the Vatican. Meanwhile, though showing signs of fatigue, he proceeded with the decoration of the Stanze. Evidence of studio work is already discernible in the *Repulsion of Attila by Leo the Great*; and in the next room, the so-called Stanza dell'Incendio, painted between 1514 and 1517, nearly all the work is by pupils. The master's hand is recognizable only in the *Burning of the Borgo*, which, however, in a certain heaviness of the chiaroscuro passages at several points, also reveals the presence of other executants.

Keeping to the tenor of the themes in the previous room, this illustrates a medieval legend which tells how, in the year 847, a fire in the Borgo (the district of Rome around the Vatican) was miraculously extinguished when Pope Leo IV appeared at a window in the Vatican Palace and made the sign of the cross. Raphael combined the episode with a classical reminiscence of the burning of Troy; hence the presence on the left of Aeneas carrying to safety his old father Anchises, followed by his son Ascanius and his wife Creusa—a symbol, certainly, of Rome and the imperial origins of the Church. The architectural setting too is in a Romanizing style, conveyed now, however, not in an evocation of space after the manner of Bramante, but rather in the taste for archaeology shown by the cornices and columns (a reflection of his new preoccupation with Roman antiquities), while forms tend to assume a sculpturesque relief.

An ideal amplification of space is here no longer attempted. Space accordingly gains in acuteness of proportions, in the accuracy of its internal relationships, in the equilibrium of its parts, with a resulting gain in the compositional freedom of the figure groups—a freedom which, however, seems to have given rise to a certain disconnectedness in the composition (probably due to the intervention of pupils). A judicious use of the Michelangelesque motif of the serpentine line imbues the figures—for example the magnificent figure of a woman in the right foreground, carrying a jar on her head—with a gracefulness and elastic vibration which, coupled with full-bodied forms, express a sense of buoyant vitality. Raphael may have been influenced too by the sinuous linework of Botticelli, with whom he shared a certain sensuousness; but while in Botticelli this disposition always verges on melancholy and eludes the grasp, as if receding into absence of mind or melting into music, in Raphael, on the contrary, it represents a state of grace, the natural accompaniment, it would seem, of pregnant sensibilities and a happy frame of mind which aspires to behold its own image in the mirror of nature.

This aspiration was realized in the decorations of the so-called Loggia, executed from about 1517 to 1519. This Loggia corresponds to the second storey of the two floors of arched galleries forming the façade of the ancient pontifical residence. This harmonious façade—which subsequently, under Gregory XIII and Sixtus V, was incorporated in the group of buildings enclosing the present Court of St Damasus—was originally designed for Julius II by Bramante, who worked on it for several years but, it seems,

RAPHAEL (1483-1520): THE BURNING OF THE BORGO, 1514-1517.
BELOW, DECORATIVE FIGURES PAINTED BY POLIDORO DA CARAVAGGIO. STANZA DELL'INCENDIO.

had scarcely begun the middle gallery when he died (in 1514). Raphael completed the façade (in 1519), maintaining its graceful equilibrium and clarity of design, and crowning it with an elegant colonnade without arches.

The Loggia decorated by Raphael forms a corridor with thirteen arcades, each containing a vault with four frescoes. In all, then, there are fifty-two scenes, most of them treating subjects from the Old Testament: this sequence is accordingly known as "Raphael's Bible." Most of the actual painting is by his pupils, but "the Loggia owes its splendour to the general order established by Raphael himself, to his critical vigilance, to his musical sense of eurythmy, to his taste, in a word to the inspired manner in which he was able to co-ordinate and, so to speak, orchestrate the highly varied talents under his direction, none of which, working on his own, ever again rose to the heights attained here" (Redig de Campos). In many cases Raphael furnished designs for the scenes, whose execution was largely delegated to Giulio Romano and Gianfrancesco Penni, assisted by Giovanni da Udine, Perino del Vaga and a whole team of minor artists whose names are given by Vasari.

THE COURT OF ST DAMASUS, WITH THE "LOGGIE," OR OPEN GALLERIES,
DESIGNED BY BRAMANTE AND RAPHAEL.

THE LOGGIA DECORATED BY RAPHAEL AND HIS PUPILS, 1517-1519.

The ornamental figures and grotesques in stucco and paints, covering the pilasters and the soffits of the arches, create a wonderfully delicate and vivacious setting within the Loggia itself: the grotesques are by Perino del Vaga and Giovanni da Udine, the stuccowork by the latter, who rediscovered the classical process of making stucco with lime and marble dust. This ornamentation comes as a delightfully fresh and vivid reminiscence of the style of classical decorations, and its model was probably the Domus Aurea or Golden House of Nero, which had then just been discovered; it reflects the interest and pleasure Raphael was taking at the time in archaeology, in his new capacity of Prefect of Antiquities in Rome.

The "Odyssey Landscapes," a work of the first century A.D. discovered on the Esquiline in the nineteenth century and now in the Vatican collections, provide a signal example of that vibrant pictorial style of Hellenistic derivation which, with its animistic

THE MIRACULOUS DRAUGHT OF FISHES (DETAIL), 1517-1519. TAPESTRY WOVEN FROM A CARTOON BY RAPHAEL. PINACOTECA VATICANA.

PERINO DEL VAGA (1500-1547) AND GIOVANNI DA UDINE (1494-1561):
CEILING DECORATION OF THE SALA DEI PONTEFICI IN THE BORGIA APARTMENT.

vitality, must have fascinated Raphael and his disciples. The narrative gusto and exuberant freshness that this type of painting conveys, the happy freedom with which the artist follows his vagrant fancies, the joyful sense of adventure expressed by the small figures abandoned to the magic embrace of nature in one of her gay and effusive moods—all this must have met with an enthusiastic reception at the blithe and lavish court of Leo X.

The rapturous enthusiasm now aroused by classical art obliterated the consciousness —so keenly felt by the early humanists—of the long intervening centuries, effaced them from the mind and relegated them to oblivion. The setting of the Biblical episodes in the Loggia is again natural scenery full of strange enchantments, a timeless, spellbound world apart. Figures seem to glide to and fro with rapt and graceful movements, as if caught up in a dance; the purity with which the compositional elements are balanced, the skill with which they are proportioned, create an all-pervading cadence and eurythmy. The aspiration—always latent in Raphael—towards a contemplative communion with nature, towards an ideality transfused and vivified through sensory responses, finds its culminating expression in the Loggia decorations in this mindless and musical accent, in the pure rapture of the rhythms, in the rhapsodic undertones of a dreamworld.

The Loggia decorations, like those in the Sistine Chapel, were the work of a team of painters, with this difference however: that in the Loggia we no longer have an alignment of works by different artists, a "chorus" in the medieval manner, attuned to the same key, but an example of teamwork for the first time in the modern sense, oriented towards a collective expression both as regards the participating artists and the arts themselves, which are here combined and blended together in varying degrees, ranging from architecture to the minor arts—the small glazed tiles of the pavement (replaced in the nineteenth century), the carved wooden doors, the stuccowork, and even the enamel-like finish (reminiscent of Pellipario majolica) of the frescoes themselves. And in its alliance of talents the Loggia reiterated and modernized the Quattrocento ideals of the Sistine Chapel—ideals dear to Raphael but henceforth remote in their mental schematism. On the poetic plane the ideals of the Sistine seem in the Loggia to have been recast and infused in a new Renaissance dream, in which the opposing poetics of Perugino and Botticelli are revived and integrated: the equilibrium and order of the first, and the psychological haziness of the second.

Raphael gladly accepted the opportunity of contributing something of his own to the physiognomy of the Sistine Chapel, and in 1515-1516 he supplied cartoons for a series of tapestries to be hung on solemn occasions along the walls of the chapel under the Quattrocento scenes of Christ and Moses. In 1517 the designs were sent to Brussels where they were woven in silk and wool in the workshops of Pieter van Aelst, who executed them with flawless technical perfection. At Christmas time, in 1519, when

RAPHAEL (1483-1520): THE TRANSFIGURATION, 1518-1520.
FINISHED BY GIULIO ROMANO AND GIANFRANCESCO PENNI. PINACOTECA VATICANA.

the finished tapestries were hung on the walls and exhibited to the *élite* of Rome, they created a sensation. The one representing the *Miraculous Draught of Fishes* is perhaps the most beautiful of them all, in the elegance of its lines, the measured harmony of the composition, in the intuitive perspective view of the waters converging towards the open horizon.

The ceiling of the Sala dei Pontefici in the Borgia Apartment, decorated under Leo X with stuccoes by Giovanni da Udine and grotesques by Perino del Vaga, has much in common with the Loggia decorations and reveals the spiritual influence of Raphael; indeed, he was probably responsible for the conception and design of the central medallion, in which Perino del Vaga represented a group of four angels, in fore-shortened perspective, whirling in a circle; here the theme of the dance is quite explicit, expressed to perfection in these gracefully swaying forms, imbued with that accent of suave and mindless rapture which runs through all Raphael's work in these years.

From this dance of angels to the upper half of the contemporary *Transfiguration*, the transition is easy, even though the latter conveys a deeper sense of poetry and—one might almost say for the first time—of speculative thought. For while even Raphael's loftiest inventions always appear to spring from pure intuition (even the mathematical relationships underlying his ideal sense of proportions and perspective are arrived at intuitively), here he seems to pause for a moment in a meditative mood whose concentration, however, suddenly dissolves into self-forgetfulness, casting the problem into the shade. This great panel was exhibited, still unfinished, at the head of Raphael's coffin. It had been commissioned in 1517 by Cardinal Giulio de' Medici for the cathedral of Narbonne. Raphael had begun work on it in July 1518, it would seem, sparing no effort to meet the express desires of his patron, "with his hand continually active," as Vasari writes. But again his pupils were destined to have a considerable share in the actual painting. When Raphael died at thirty-seven, on the 6th of April 1520, he had scarcely done more than sketch in the figures in the lower half of the picture (whereas the upper part was virtually complete). It was therefore left to Giulio Romano and Gianfrancesco Penni to finish the work; they are responsible for the heavy chiaroscuro, which forms too strong a contrast (a contrast perhaps intended, within certain limits, by the master himself) with the unearthly lightness of the upper scene.

Raphael followed the account of the Transfiguration given in the Gospel of St Matthew. Above the mountain top appears the radiant figure of Christ, soaring in the air, as Moses and Elias descend towards Him. On the ground below are Peter, James and John, stirring with slow and musical gestures, as they rouse themselves from their torpor. The great cloud of light seems to absorb and give back an attenuated echo of the encircling cadences of this celestial dance. The musicality of the Loggia decorations has here been transposed into a more ethereal rhythm which neither conceals nor deflects its potency, but tempers and softens it until it approximates to immateriality.

Technical virtuosity now takes the upper hand, as had been the case with Michelangelo in his *Pietà*. And singularly enough, with both Michelangelo and Raphael, the object of this virtuosity is to carry form to an extreme, to a sublime pitch of refinement—an aim only to be achieved by degrees, through a sequence of subtle transitions which only a superlative virtuoso technique could render. And just as Michelangelo's *Pietà* anticipates academicism, so Raphael here, in the *Transfiguration*, directly prefigures the "sublime" of Guido Reni—a spirituality which, though purified of their taint, springs ultimately from the senses.

Raphael died in 1520. In less than two years Leo X followed him to the grave. His successor was Adrian VI (1522-1523), whose brief and austere reign lasted but twenty months. Then came the stormy, war-torn pontificate of Clement VII (1523-1534) who, in the turmoil of politics, had little time to devote to art; now, in 1527, occurred the terrible sack of Rome by German mercenary troops. Clement was succeeded by Paul III (1534-1549), energetic instigator of the Catholic restoration.

The reform movement launched in Germany by Martin Luther had gained ground rapidly. At the time of Clement's death in 1534, England, Denmark, Sweden and vast areas of Germany and Switzerland had renounced their allegiance to the pope. The efforts of the Church to arrest the progress of Protestantism came to be known as the Counter-Reformation; it entered its most active phase in the second half of the sixteenth century, under the stimulus of the Council of Trent (1545-1563). The Church redefined the orthodox faith and systematically refuted the tenets of the Lutheran heresy. It sought to restore morality, particularly among the clergy, by laying down and enforcing stricter standards of conduct; at the same time it enjoined the laity at large to observe the moral precepts and dogmas of the Catholic faith, on pain of purgatorial punishment.

Mournful, cerebral and repentant, the Counter-Reformation is reflected in these very colours in certain aspects of Mannerist painting. But when we look for the authentic spokesman of those anxious moral aspirations which the Counter-Reformation crystallized in its theological doctrines, of that mystical impulse which, thwarted by the breakdown of humanist ideals and by the hard political and historical realities of the age, manifested itself in obscure misgivings—when we look for that spokesman, we find him in Michelangelo.

The easy-going optimism of Leo X was no longer justifiable. The conditions that had favoured the triumph of Raphael had been transformed. It was Michelangelo's hour, and his figure now looms up without a rival over the Roman art world. From 1536 to 1541 he painted the *Last Judgement* in the Sistine Chapel. From 1542 to 1550 he painted the fresco decorations of the Pauline Chapel. From 1546 until his death in 1564 he acted as chief architect of St Peter's, supervising the construction of the new basilica.

MICHELANGELO (1475-1564): THE LAST JUDGEMENT, 1536-1541. FRESCO IN THE SISTINE CHAPEL.

In 1533, shortly before his death, Clement VII had asked Michelangelo to paint a fresco of the *Last Judgement* on the wall behind the altar of the Sistine Chapel, and another of the *Fall of the Rebel Angels* on the opposite wall, over the entrance (the latter was never carried beyond the planning stage); and the artist accordingly prepared a design. When Paul III mounted the papal throne in the following year, he enthusiastically approved the idea and Michelangelo went to work.

Henceforth the ideal of harmony expressed in the Quattrocento architecture and decorations of the Sistine Chapel was disregarded. A quarter of a century before, Michelangelo had endeavoured to adapt his ceiling frescoes to the architectonic structure of the chapel, and had found in Plato an ideological link—although a profoundly disturbing one—with the pre-existing frescoes. But now there was no attempt at adaptation, no effort to establish a link with the previous work. The vast wall surface was cleared (in 1535) of its original decorations by Perugino (even two lunettes of Michelangelo's own series of the *Ancestors of Christ* were destroyed), the windows were bricked up, and he proceeded to cover the wall entirely with the new fresco, working alone, unassisted, from the summer of 1536 to the autumn of 1541. The fresco is devoid of any architectonic setting; the picture space is nowhere conceived in relation to the chapel itself, nor has it any articulation or orientation in terms of perspective: it is like a great void in which a mass of bodies are suspended.

Against a uniform background of open sky, of a turgid blue devoid of transparencies, the figures stand out in sombre, muddy-coloured tonalities. The colours may have darkened with the passage of time, but this sombreness was to a large extent the very effect intended by the artist. One of the weapons of the Counter-Reformation was awe and terror, and Michelangelo availed himself gladly of the opportunity to pour his soul into an Apocalyptic vision of Judgement, acting on the spectator like a nightmare—the projection of his own *terribilità*, his stern yet passionate violence of temper.

The finalism expressed by the conception of the ceiling fresco springs from the representation of a conflict between mind and matter, between body and soul—a conflict that magnifies man, as he strives for liberation. In the *Last Judgement*, this finalism gives way, resolving itself negatively into the acknowledgement of a supreme fatality which, for all his titanic exertions, man is powerless to overrule or abate. Now that the Counter-Reformation, in exalting theology at the expense of philosophy, had upset the balance achieved by the Renaissance between revealed Truth and rational Truth, philosophy in Michelangelo's eyes ceased to have any positive value; thought, too, was powerless and unarmed. With these intellectual defences down, there sprang up the vivid sense of a primordial, irreducible anguish, whose accents now were no longer painfully cerebral, but deeper than that—almost visceral. Rapt before by the quickening, liberating afflatus of the ceiling fresco, here, with the *Last Judgement* before him, the spectator is dazed and overwhelmed by the rumble, as it were, of confused and mighty sounds, whose echo dies away in caverns "measureless to man," while there rings in his ears the raucous blast of the trumpets blown by the angels who form the lower pivot of the composition (the upper coinciding with the figure of the Almighty).

The longed-for consolations of philosophy afforded Michelangelo no relief, nor was any to be found in religion. Since the hopes born of a finalistic doctrine were always frustrated by a fate threatening and fearful in its workings, God for him was no longer the supreme goal of all aspirations, the pledge of spiritual liberation, but the very image of that threat and that fearfulness. Here is a God that does not pardon but requires expiation. His raised right arm motions the Blessed upward, his left consigns the Damned to their doom in the underworld. With slow and majestic rhythms the composition circles round this pivot, this image of Aristotle's "motionless mover," this metaphor (as it might be called on the strength of the Apollonian figuration of the Almighty, here again a Christ-Helios in the Early Christian tradition exemplified also in the Vatican necropolis) which anticipates by some years the heliocentric conception of Copernicus.

On the lower left is the resurrection of the dead. "A livid sky extends above the shattered earth, which seems to be vomiting up the shapeless bodies to which it had given asylum for so long. Their incomplete torsos are like lumps of earth painfully breaking free of the mire" (Tolnay). Above, in a zone where the earth's force of gravity is no longer exerted and where the celestial force of attraction is still weak, a welter of nudes whirls through the void, their bodies swollen rather than sculptural, like the eerie figments of some fearful dream. This space, in fact, is like the psychic world of incubi, all hovering there tormentedly without hope of release. It might almost be a transposition of Dante's image of "those who are suspended." Such a suggestion may even have taken effect on the artist without any intentional identification with the souls in Purgatory. But we find what is certainly an explicit reference to the *Divine Comedy* in the figure on the lower right of Charon ferrying the Damned, who are huddled together behind Minos, supreme judge of the underworld.

There is no philosophical superstructure here but a wholly theological one, for the sources are no longer the thinkers of antiquity but the Holy Scriptures and Dante, hailed in his own century as *theologus* and included by Raphael among the theologians in the *Disputa*. Along with philosophy, the artist has also repudiated classicism, which, in the equilibrium achieved by the Renaissance between revealed and natural Truth, had been reconciled with the Christian world, but which now the Counter-Reformation identified negatively with paganism. The very notion of non-perspective space must have seemed distinctly anti-classical; furthermore the figures, as if deformed by the surging currents of this empty space, are elongated and compressed, doing violence to the classical canon of proportions. Their swollen forms are no longer the sculpturesque expression of an internal plastic tension, but seem to expand under the action

MICHELANGELO (1475-1564): THE BLESSED, DETAIL OF THE LAST JUDGEMENT, 1536-1541. FRESCO IN THE SISTINE CHAPEL.

MICHELANGELO (1475-1564): THE CONVERSION OF ST PAUL (DETAIL), 1542-1550. FRESCO IN THE PAULINE CHAPEL.

VIEW OF THE PAULINE CHAPEL, BUILT BY ANTONIO DA SANGALLO THE YOUNGER ABOUT 1540.

of some obscure fermentation. Masses have no structural organization, and the chiaroscuro, instead of emphasizing anatomical features, blurs and confuses them. A thick coat of soot covers the bodies like a cloak, and through this foggy obscurity they seem to be groping for their way and for their destiny.

Even before the *Last Judgement* was finished, Paul III had a further commission for Michelangelo—which was, to decorate the new chapel built for the pope after 1537 by Antonio da Sangallo the Younger. Severely classical in its sober lines and compact ground-plan, the chapel was redecorated, after the fire of 1545, with heavy stucco ornaments as a substitute for the original stuccoes, surely of more graceful design, furnished by Perino del Vaga. From 1542 to 1550 Michelangelo worked in the Pauline Chapel on the two frescoes, on facing walls, representing the *Conversion of St Paul* and the *Crucifixion of St Peter*. Here the anti-classical tendency of the *Last Judgement* is even more pronounced.

The clustered groups of ghostly figures seem to exist in a kind of mysterious communion with the bleak landscape around them, a waste land whose woolly outlines dissolve into the ashen background of the sky. The dramatic events taking place make no impression on these sluggish, almost flaccid figures. What stirs and impels them, on the contrary, is an internal flux, hermetically outlined in the tortuous, long drawn out development of the composition, like an echo telepathically transmitted from one figure to another; together they hearken to a voice from above, which comes down to them through the heavy layers of the atmosphere, and on which their destiny depends.

Now it is a voice that does not accuse or condemn, but soothes and pardons. It reveals itself (before it is too late) as the only hope of salvation in the slow shipwreck of time. Michelangelo was an old man. The final, almost blasphemous revolt of the *Last Judgement*—the passive revolt of a rebel maddened by his own failure—gave place to a resigned and uncomplaining humility. Michelangelo was chastising his own Titanism, expiating the sin of pride, the last of his sins to be rooted out (now that, in his old age, the hold of the senses had weakened) and also the most reluctant to recognize and confess itself as such.

True, there is a sense of impending doom, calling for expiation, contrition and self-sacrifice, but this doom identifies itself now, once again, with a positive finality, for the expiation takes place on earth, not in eternal damnation. And out of the sore distress of expiation comes salvation; the error lies precisely in revolt. Here, it seems to me, is the substance of Michelangelo's religious "conversion," which in these years had been maturing under the influence of his passionate friendship with Vittoria Colonna, and which inevitably brought to a close the stormy spiritual pilgrimage of one who had always yearned for the peace and moral fulfilment of the Faith.

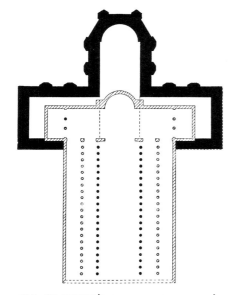

OLD ST PETER'S WITH ROSSELLINO'S
PROJECTED APSE AND TRANSEPT.

PLANS FOR ST PETER'S

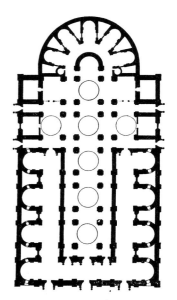

FRA GIOCONDO'S PLAN.

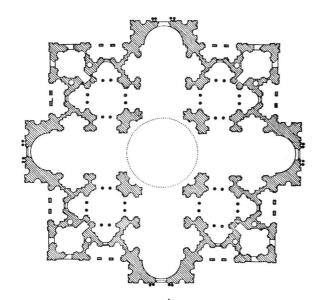

BRAMANTE'S PLAN.

PERUZZI'S PLAN (AFTER SERLIO).

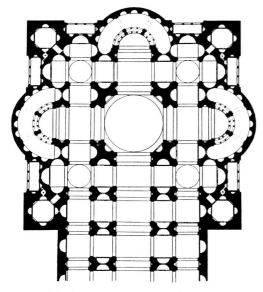

RECONSTRUCTION BY FÖRSTER
OF BRAMANTE'S FINAL PLAN.

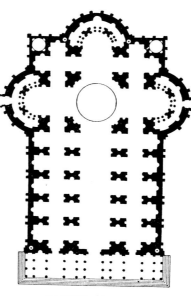

RAPHAEL'S PLAN.

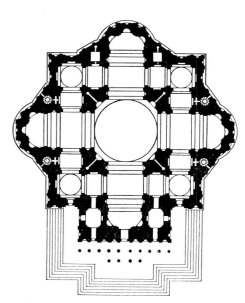

MICHELANGELO'S PLAN.

The crowning achievement of Michelangelo's long years of work in the Vatican was the completion of St Peter's. The progress made in the construction of the new basilica can be summarized as follows. Shortly before his death in 1514, Bramante designated Raphael as his successor in the post of chief architect of St Peter's. Working in collaboration with Fra Giocondo and Giuliano da Sangallo, Raphael drew up a plan which kept essentially to Bramante's project, with certain modifications. For one thing, the reduced size of the niches gave the new plan a less organic character, more in keeping with Raphael's own distributive and proportional conception of space. But his chief modification lay in lengthening the nave, thus converting Bramante's central plan (in the form of a Greek cross) into a longitudinal plan (in the form of a Latin cross). In taking this step Raphael was certainly acting at the instigation of the ecclesiastical authorities, who were anxious to have a church spacious enough to accommodate the great religious ceremonies.

Under Raphael the work of construction made very little progress. After his death (in 1520), Baldassare Peruzzi was appointed to replace him as "master of the works." He submitted a further ground-plan, again in the form of a Greek cross, inspired by Bramante's original conception—but with some vital differences. Owing to preoccupations of a static order (which Bramante, with his exceptional technical skill, would

WOODEN MODEL OF ANTONIO DA SANGALLO'S PROJECT FOR ST PETER'S.

FRESCO OF ABOUT 1588 SHOWING THE OBELISK IN ST PETER'S SQUARE
AND THE PORTICO OF OLD ST PETER'S. VATICAN LIBRARY.

The Egyptian obelisk in the foreground, which once stood in the Circus of Nero, was set up here, in the square in front of St Peter's, by Domenico Fontana at the behest of Sixtus V in 1586. Visible in the background is the mighty drum of Michelangelo's dome, still in process of construction; it was finished by Fontana between 1588 and 1590. It was Fontana, too, who in 1588 built the great Sistine Hall of the new library, of whose decorations this fresco forms part. The east end of Old St Peter's shown here (demolished a few years after this picture was painted) includes the pointed top of the façade, just visible behind the portico, and the fifteenth century Loggia delle Benedizioni (to the right of the obelisk). Rising high on the right are the Loggie of Bramante and Raphael, forming an angle with the new wing added by Gregory XIII (1572-1585); to this Sixtus V (1585-1590) added still another wing, thus forming the present Court of St Damasus.

have made light of), Peruzzi increased the size of all the junctures and piers, with the result that full spaces seemed to prevail over empty ones. The clarity of the original plan had been lost.

On Peruzzi's death (in 1537), Paul III put Antonio da Sangallo the Younger in charge of building operations, the architect who had just designed the Pauline Chapel in the Vatican. The wooden model prepared by Sangallo is still extant. He maintained the Greek cross, but extended it in front with a large portico. The external features proposed by Sangallo were inspired by the orders of the Colosseum and the Theatre of Marcellus. On the whole, the project is confused and over-elaborate, and fails to allow for adequate lighting within. Michelangelo objected to it and when, on Sangallo's death (in 1546), he himself became chief architect of St Peter's, he set it aside at once.

PIRRO LIGORIO (C. 1500-1583): THE CASINO, OR SUMMER HOUSE, OF POPE PIUS IV, 1558-1562. VATICAN GARDENS.

CEILING DECORATIONS BY PROSPERO ORSI IN THE SISTINE HALL OF THE VATICAN LIBRARY.

Michelangelo reverted to the central plan of Bramante, and to his general conception. But by embodying the outlying parts of the building in a continuously developing, structurally compact design, he obtained a more robust, better organized edifice. The play of forces within, instead of being broken up into isolated elements, develops in continuous interaction from the mighty piers to the peripheral masses, whose size denotes the tensions at work. And all these forces, in the grip of the gravitational attraction of matter, converge on the pendentives and ribs of the dome, and from there are channelled upward, as if finally set free.

When Michelangelo died (in 1564), the north and south arms of the transept were nearly finished, and with them a substantial portion of the drum on which the dome was to rest; and the west apse had been begun. The dome itself and the lantern above it were built to his designs between 1588 and 1590.

THE SISTINE HALL OF THE VATICAN LIBRARY, BUILT BY DOMENICO FONTANA IN 1588.

THE DOME OF ST PETER'S, DESIGNED BY MICHELANGELO.

Michelangelo's initial successor as chief architect of St Peter's was Pirro Ligorio. The Casino, or summer house, which he erected in the Vatican gardens, begun for Paul IV (1555-1559) and completed under Pius IV (1559-1565), displays the elegance and fanciful verve of his inspiration; the decorations, combining stuccowork, frescoes and inlays, are conceived in a spirit of antiquarian whimsicality faintly reminiscent of the Vatican Loggia decorated by Raphael and his pupils. Ligorio's style is one of brilliant but superficial brio, with an affected compositional equilibrium which already seems to point the way to the impeccable suavity of neo-classicism. These are the qualities that made it impossible for him to rise to the severe and lordly heights of Michelangelo's conceptions. Ligorio was eager to revise and modify Michelangelo's project for the new St Peter's, but he met with so much opposition that, after the death of Pius V (in 1572), he was dismissed and Domenico Fontana appointed in his stead.

Fontana was an architect of great technical skill and resourcefulness. To him Sixtus V (1585-1590) entrusted the very difficult task of removing the great Egyptian obelisk from where it lay in the Circus of Nero and setting it up in front of St Peter's (1586), where it still stands. For the same pope Fontana designed and built the new seat of the Vatican Library, in the court of the Belvedere. The main vaulted hall, divided by six piers into two naves richly decorated with colourful frescoes in the Mannerist style, reveals an unquestionable capacity for the practical organization of space—space characterized, however, not so much by architectonic qualities as by the vivid life of its polychrome ornamentation. An architect like Fontana, who on the whole was a technician, deeply versed in static problems, rather than a personality, was at this juncture the very man required to carry out Michelangelo's designs for the dome without deviating from them in any essential particular.

In fact the construction of the great dome, under the direction of Fontana, keeps more closely than is commonly supposed to the spirit of the project finally worked out by Michelangelo, who had given years of thought to the problem, weighing the relative merits of a hemispherical dome and a tall, elongated cupola. He finally elected for the latter form, whose soaring lines, moreover, seem to re-echo the mystical longings of his old age; and to this conception Fontana largely adhered, only accentuating the external height of the dome.

The mighty upward thrust of the dome collects and mobilizes the structural forces powerfully compressed into the lower body of the edifice, making them converge on a culminating point at the top, where the lantern rises above the main dome, like an ideal, inaccessible temple apart, dwarfed by the distance at which it is seen from the ground below. The vertical sweep of dome and lantern by no means detracts from the vigour and plenitude of their volumes, but is perfectly consistent with them, finding its full expression in the tension of the ribs ascending towards the focal point formed by the lantern.

CARAVAGGIO (1573-1610): THE DEPOSITION, ABOUT 1602-1604. PINACOTECA VATICANA.

5

THE BAROQUE AFTERMATH

The Counter-Reformation, in upsetting the balance achieved by the High Renaissance between Christianity and classicism, marked in effect a return to a mystical form of religion. But the wide freedom of thought and outlook acquired and exercised by men as a result of the Renaissance, could not now be reabsorbed in a transcendental faith of the medieval type. Medieval faith, which dissolved sensory and emotional responses in a pure metaphysical aspiration, could not be rekindled.

As we have seen in the previous chapter, philosophical thought had evolved towards a kind of pantheistic naturalism (also shared, though in very different ways, by such artists as Leonardo and Raphael) which attributed a cognitive function not only to reason but also to the senses; and which sought, not in a transcendental but rather in an immanent vision, for the meeting point between man and God, between the finite and the infinite, between the particular and the universal. This was the line of thought which, as already noted, took its rise with Nicholas of Cusa, was developed by Bernardino Telesio and came to a head in Giordano Bruno (1548-1600). The new mystical impulse could not but be conditioned by these philosophical premises and develop in a direction wholly consistent with them; indeed, far from transcending the world of the senses, it could not help but adapt itself to that world and draw sustenance from it.

St Ignatius Loyola (1491-1556), founder of the Society of Jesus, was also the moving spirit behind this new mysticism, which left its mark on Baroque art—a mysticism of ecstatic rapture and sensuous visions. Reason and the senses were the attributes of man to which humanism had attached particular importance; and while Luther laid stress on reason, intent as he was on stripping religion of every supposed superfluity in order to shed the clearest, most unequivocal light on the word of God, St Ignatius on the other hand, the anti-Lutheran *par excellence*, laid the emphasis on irrationality, in pursuance of a religion wholly compounded of visions and inner intuitions. St Ignatius opted for a form of irrationality based on the senses, which found its counterpart in the fantasies of Baroque art and architecture.

Needless to say, this mystical attitude by no means implied a hedonistic indulgence in mere sensory responses; these tended to be transcended. But they remained the point of departure, the stimulus towards asceticism, from which that asceticism took its restless and impassioned, its troubled and visionary character. Troubled in the sense that it has little or none of that ideal limpidity, that crystalline transparency of thought which had characterized, for example, the intensely religious vision of Fra Angelico. But now, after the collapse of the humanist myth, the religious attitude of Fra Angelico was a thing of the past, irretrievable and unrenewable. And it was at this very time that Vasari came forward with his misleading interpretation of Fra Angelico as an inspired visionary recording his miraculous glimpses of another world.

The intense and transcendent mysticism of St Ignatius is a form of the sublimation of the senses. But before they can be sublimated, the senses must be chastised (which is to say, in effect, quickened and sharpened) through abstinence and mortification of the body. Under this aspect, the vision of St Ignatius Loyola is not unconnected with that of his contemporary Michelangelo. What the latter has in common with St Ignatius is his obsession with evil, his anguished and harassing sense of sin; the Titanism of Michelangelo and the grandiose, ambitious character of the actions and affirmations of St Ignatius have this in common too, that they both represent an aspiration towards catharsis. But while for Michelangelo the soul, imprisoned in the body, was still the Platonic soul, yearning for a pure though unattainable world of ideas, for St Ignatius the soul was indissolubly bound to the body, interwoven with its very fibers, torn between the senses and the passions but also directly expressing them.

Once the most contrite and rigorous phase of the Counter-Reformation had passed, Baroque mysticism proceeded to identify the soul with the senses, intuition or religious illumination with fantasy, and to identify them even more fully and with a more impassioned (though no longer anguished) restlessness than ever before. The sensuous character of religious ecstasy, which found a typical expression in Bernini's famous *St Teresa*, now became more explicit. The triumph of lights and colours, in an open and shifting space freely traversed by the flux of sensations, expressed at the same time the glorious yearnings of the soul and the surrender of the senses and fancy. At this point the ascetic and imaginative faith of St Ignatius was united with, and corrected by, the pantheistic ideology and cosmic naturalism of Giordano Bruno. Bernini became the official spokesman and the loftiest interpreter of this new vision.

We have already noted in Quattrocento art a conflict between religious and secular tendencies. But even the secular tendencies were sustained by a divine faith in man, and in the end this conflict was resolved, in the great myth of the Renaissance, in an aulic reconciliation between philosophy and theology. Michelangelo was the first to undermine the foundations of that myth. Man, raised to the status of a Titan and measuring himself with God, had come off humbled from the encounter, and God had acquired, in the *Last Judgement,* a threatening aspect. It was God who held possession of man. The new mysticism of St Ignatius provided man with a means of regaining possession of God.

But his attitude and approach failed to satisfy those who shrank from mysticism and were inclined to be critical-minded; for them the quest of God was fraught with anxieties, even with despair. Such was the case with Caravaggio. Rejecting the neo-mysticism of St Ignatius and his peculiar compromise between immanence and transcendence, Caravaggio remained attached to a kind of immanence doctrine which no longer had the confident and positive accents of Renaissance thought, but which came, rather, as a hypothetical quantity requiring to be tried and tested. To test and confirm it, for Caravaggio, was not a rational process, but an instinctive, dramatically conducted investigation, an anxious search into the nature of things, forcing him almost to grope for his way, with profound insights which, however, were always overshadowed by doubts.

God had become, as it were, a question mark. The sense of mystery with which Leonardo, engrossed in a quest of knowledge centred on man, had surrounded the problem of God, was transformed by Caravaggio—now that that central interest had waned—into an all-pervading sense of doubt, into an all-embracing passion for research and investigation, always centred, however, by the force of his tendential subjectivism, on natural data. His naturalism, in fact, was quickened and intensified into outright realism. The theme of reality was one that he drove home with stubborn insistence, but he always sought to penetrate through the strata of reality, with cutting edges of light, to an underlying essence of truth. The anguish of Michelangelo sprang from an obsession with sin, the restlessness of Caravaggio from obsessive doubts.

Caravaggio's vision, as instinctively expressed in painting, appears to have points of contact with the philosophical views of Giordano Bruno. His early works are for the most part genre pictures, ironic and almost insolent in their undisguised paganism, marked by a brazen naturalism that puts the accent on physical sensations; they reveal a sceptical, materialistic outlook, which however failed to satisfy him for long, though it continued for years to characterize the psychological atmosphere of his paintings. Bruno too passed through a materialistic phase, which he abandoned for a pantheistic conception of God, whom he identifies with the infinitude and animation of the universe and nature. In Caravaggio the pressure of anxiety and doubt is more urgent and substantial than it is in Bruno, an essentially religious spirit, whose doubts concerned not God so much as the Christian dogma.

Caravaggio rejected the mental apriorism and the ideal models of Mannerist painting. With what at the time was an almost revolutionary volte-face he took nature as his model. When he was exhorted to study the statues of Pheidias and Glycon, writes his biographer Bellori, he merely "pointed with his hand towards a crowd of persons near by, thus indicating that nature had sufficiently provided him with masters." He would have agreed with Bruno when the philosopher wrote that "nature should be the measure of reason, not reason of nature."

In trying to grasp the underlying significance of Caravaggio's luminist, naturalistic style, at the point where, without being deliberately conceptual, it coincides with a new conception of the world, we find useful guidance in Bruno's principle of "omni-form substance," in which the distinction between mind and matter "is reduced to a being and a root": substance becomes tangible by increasing and extending itself; but in doing so "it does not take its dimensions as if from outside, but transmits and drives them out as if from the centre." Caravaggio seems to have been inspired by a similar intuition: light, in his paintings, becomes tangible by virtually expressing, in itself, the physical substance of bodies.

Caravaggio's light does not irradiate the figures, nor is it radiated or emitted *by* the figures, as it was, for example, in the *Angel delivering St Peter* by Raphael, in which light opposes its immaterial substance to the physical substance of bodies. With Caravaggio, on the contrary, light comes into existence together with bodies; it has no external source, it is abstract and material at once. In Raphael, the sensible and the intelligible, while reconciled with each other, remain distinct: geometry (i.e. the Idea or the reflection of it) gave form and order, "as if from outside," to nature. In Caravaggio's light, on the other hand, there is no distinction between the material and the spiritual, between the idea and the senses, but perfect identity between the abstract and the concrete. Contraries coincide and merge into that unity dear to Bruno with his theory of monism.

Light and its opposite number, shadow, are also made to coincide and merge into unity. Light is integrated into shadow, as the full into the empty, the finite into the infinite; light partakes of shadow, as the finite partakes of the infinite, and in it finds its explanation.

Moreover, the objection that Caravaggio seems to make to the clear and uniform luminosity, meridian and shadowless, peculiar to Renaissance art, and coinciding with a wide open picture space receding in perspective, is comparable to the objection that Bruno—on the analogy, as it so happened, of light and shade—had made to the traditional conception of God as an abstract and transcendental being. God, according to him, cannot be "absolute, incomprehensible light but rather its shadow, the world, the universe, the nature within things."

CARAVAGGIO (1573-1610): THE DEPOSITION (DETAIL), ABOUT 1602-1604. PINACOTECA VATICANA.

It is shadow that explains light, and the infinite that explains the finite. Thus Caravaggio abolished the perspective framework of Renaissance painting, whereby bodies were located in space, in order to define their positions solely by means of contrasting shadow and light, without (or almost without) any fixed point of reference in terms of perspective. After Michelangelo's *Last Judgement* (which anticipated this development), here was the first and deepest reflection in art of that conception of space as an infinite extension, which Bruno had deduced from the new cosmology of Copernicus, squarely opposed to the traditional geocentric cosmology. And in his final, most dramatic phase, Caravaggio deepened and extended the zone of shadow, making it coincide with great empty spaces, where the allusion to the infinite becomes more direct.

Bruno's conception of an infinite space is embodied much more explicitly (and more superficially) in Baroque art, in a continuous vision, multiform in its application of perspective and without any definition of limits. It is a conception of space in which every centre is relative, space being equally occupied by an infinite amount of matter moved by the same intrinsic cause that forms and rotates innumerable worlds. And while Baroque came into its own in this new vision of the world, with a joyful, sensual upsurge of unclouded optimism, Caravaggio seemed to be well aware, with an uneasiness and pessimism such as Bruno himself had never felt, of the confusion and dramatic plight in which man found himself, now that the geocentric theory of the universe was discounted and he had lost for good the comforting conviction of standing at the very centre of things.

The cosmic anxiety that Michelangelo, a few years in advance of Copernicus' discoveries, already seemed to express in the empty space, devoid of perspective and of any outlet, of his *Last Judgement*, reappears in Caravaggio, but more deeply ingrained in the consciousness and reabsorbed in his thought—in other words more deeply rooted and ramified. It was not, as with Michelangelo, a fresh anguish growing out of an older one, but came as an integral part of his anxious state of mind; of doubts as to what lay beyond the thick curtain of shadow, which might conceal the infinite or nothingness, God or blind necessity; of actions arrested (as in the Vatican *Deposition*) in a tragic suspension that seems to harbour both silence and clamour, the throbbing pulse of the present and the echo of the ages. And the more intense the realism, the higher the degree of abstraction. The more remote God is, the more anxiously is he sought for.

If the universe is infinite and we ourselves are in the infinite, God cannot be outside the infinite but within it, within the things that partake of the infinite; and within ourselves, wherein lies, in fact, that anxious fear of the infinite and that aspiration towards it. But while for Bruno that anxiety is simply a proof of the existence of God, Caravaggio seems at heart to oscillate between this solution and the opposite one, which is, that that anxiety is the symptom of man's abandonment and loneliness, and of the non-existence of God.

This underlying content of his vision—for the rankling anxiety inherent in the very aspect of his painting, so unlike anything that had gone before, must have struck even those who were puzzled by it—is in itself sufficient to account for the opposition Caravaggio met with in ecclesiastical circles. And it accounts for that opposition better than the reasons usually adduced: the alleged indecency and vulgarity of his style, or its excessive realism—a realism whose significance was in any case inseparable from that content.

In the very year (1600), or a few months after, in which Giordano Bruno was burned at the stake as a heretic in the Campo dei Fiori in Rome, Caravaggio painted a *Conversion of St Paul* for the church of Santa Maria del Popolo whose iconography must then have seemed almost shocking in its novelty and also in its probable allusions to the pantheistic naturalism of Bruno. The figure of God is nowhere to be seen. St Paul is lying on his back, blinded by a shaft of divine light whose irruption from above is very vaguely indicated; indeed it seems rather to be issuing—and this is a brilliant stroke of poetic invention on the artist's part—from the broad flank of the horse at whose feet the saint has fallen, and which turns its head towards him with an intensely speaking gaze. The figure of the horse seems to take the place of that of God, or anyhow to serve as its intermediate agent.

Caravaggio was a rebel, in open revolt against society, and in this he was upheld not only by his pride but by a reckless insolence which, psychologically, might well explain the attraction he felt not so much for the ideas behind the Protestant heresy as, perhaps, for the mere act of heresy itself, as a manifestation of nonconformity. Walter Friedländer has thrown light on his contacts with the Congregation of the Oratory, founded by St Philip Neri, whose religious ideas had been suspected, particularly under Pius V, of being tainted with Lutheranism; Caravaggio must have sympathized both with the intense and humble simplicity of their warm religious sentiments, no doubt thoroughly congenial to him, a man of the people, and with their keen dislike of official rules and regulations.

The *Deposition*, which entered the Vatican gallery in the nineteenth century, was originally painted from about 1602 to 1604 for the church of the Oratorians, Santa Maria in Vallicella. Here the compact masses are regrouped in a single block of light, suspended, on the edge of the open tomb, as if on the abyss of death. The drama seems to have no alternative but the void, the abyss, the unknown. Only the overt, forlorn gesture of one of the Marys evades that alternative, breaking the spell and appealing for succour from on high.

For St Peter's Caravaggio painted a large canvas, the so-called *Madonna of the Serpent*. Datable to about 1605-1606, this work was commissioned by the Confraternity of the Ostlers for its altar in the Vatican basilica. The Virgin and Child are represented in

CARAVAGGIO (1573-1610): THE MADONNA OF THE SERPENT, ABOUT 1605-1606. BORGHESE GALLERY, ROME.

the act of crushing the serpent, symbol of evil and heresy; beside them stands St Anne, patroness of the Confraternity, a rude, sunburnt, peasant-like figure, majestic in her rugged force. According to Baglione, the painting was removed from the altar by order of Cardinal Della Fabbrica and given to Cardinal Scipione Borghese (it is still in the Borghese Collection today). Bellori adds that it was removed on account of the vulgarity of the representation. Friedländer has recently suggested that the real reason was simply its inordinate size (9½ by nearly 7 feet), which made it ill-adapted to the altar for which it was intended.

Then there is the further circumstance that the theme of this picture was a particularly delicate one, for it was based on texts whose interpretation had given rise to a controversy between Catholics and Protestants. Where the former read *ipsa*, thus attributing to the Virgin the action of crushing the serpent (i.e. stamping out evil), the latter read *ipse* and attributed the action to the Son. Pope Pius V (1566-1572) had sought to reconcile the two points of view by issuing a Bull, to the effect that the serpent was crushed by the Virgin but with the help of the Son.

A painting of the sixteenth century, by Figino, already shows the Child placing his small foot on that of Mary, as together they crush the snake. Subsequent paintings by Cignani, Rubens and Maratta lay particular stress on the action of the Virgin, while the part played by the Child, though handled with various degrees of acuteness and circumspection, was minimized. Lomazzo's initial interpretation of the theme, which observed the Bull of Pius V to the letter, was therefore revised and brought closer to the version preferred by Catholics.

Now Caravaggio not only took over the iconography of Lomazzo, but by placing the figure of the Infant Jesus in the foreground, in full light, he in effect laid the predominant emphasis on the role played by Christ, thus laying himself open to the charge (which indeed may well have been justified) of leaning towards the Protestant interpretation of this controversial theme. This in itself would have been reason enough for the removal of the picture from St Peter's, the very sanctuary and stronghold of Catholicism. For each new work of art which found a place in St Peter's in these years was carefully chosen and answered a specific doctrinal purpose in the Church's conflict with the Protestant heresy.

The Protestants denied that St Peter had died in Rome and that Christ had chosen him as the head of the Church; they therefore refused to acknowledge the authority of the Pope. It was for this reason that, when the surviving eastern portions of Old St Peter's were torn down in 1607-1612, care was taken to preserve such works as Giotto's "Navicella" mosaic, in which St Peter is singled out by Christ as the leader of the Church, and Filarete's bronze door, which celebrates the conception of the *Ecclesia imperialis*. To Filarete's door was now added, to strengthen the argument, a bas-relief of *Christ entrusting the Christian Flock to St Peter*. Early in the seventeenth century, with the same purpose in mind, the Church ordered from different artists a series of pictures representing episodes in the life of the Chief Apostle.

Among these was the *Crucifixion of St Peter* by Guido Reni, executed at the very beginning of the new century. Reni definitely comes forward here as a kind of anti-Caravaggio. He borrows the latter's emphatic chiaroscuro effects, and even his composition, though differing in some respects, distinctly reflects Caravaggio's interpretation of the same subject in the picture in Santa Maria del Popolo. Here again, as in Caravaggio, we find the bare feet and calves of the executioners in the foreground; so it was not such "vulgar" details as this so much as the underlying substance of his conception that aroused so much opposition to Caravaggio's paintings. And it was in the merit and substance of the work that Reni set out to contradict Caravaggio, with the polemical intention of showing how, with the same interplay of light and shade, and the same realistic fidelity of observation, the artist might express a vision which, to Reni's thinking, was less equivocal and more worthy of the sacredness of the theme.

Shadow here is not, as in Caravaggio, dense and compact, nor does it conceal any lurking doubts or questionings, but gradually thins out over a landscape. This is not abstract but naturalistic shadow, crepuscular or nocturnal, atmospheric and vaporous. Nature as depicted here, however, aspires to the sublime through a refinement of the tangible in the ideal: light comes as the culminating accent of this gradual ascent to the sublime. Action is not, as in Caravaggio, harshly locked and arrested; it is disengaged and free, but at the same time sublimated in an extreme slowness of motion.

Caravaggio modelled himself directly on nature. With Reni, on the other hand, nature is corrected and recast in accordance with an ideal archetype harking back to classical statuary and to Raphael. Gestures are measured, forms are elongated and modulated, and tapered, as in the *Apollo Belvedere*, the much admired copy in the Vatican of a Greek original of the fourth century B.C. But movements are much more sinuous, more smoothly articulated in their agitation. The reminiscence of the dance that the later Raphael embodies in his figures is repeated by Guido Reni, but in much more enfeebled forms and without the sweetness and felicity of Raphael.

All Reni's work was produced after the rupture of the Renaissance equilibrium, whereas Raphael stood at the very centre of that equilibrium. The latter saw nature as harmonious, untrammelled and vibrant, but governed by a clear geometric pattern: the well-defined rules of perspective and proportions. This was the "idea" of Raphael, immanent in all things, like a reflection of God. The "idea" that Guido Reni pursued was, on the contrary, something continually longed for, but undefined and unattained. Lacking any precise objective or final goal, his aspiration to the sublime ended (particularly in his later period, which marks his highest achievement) by consisting merely

GUIDO RENI (1575-1642): THE CRUCIFIXION OF ST PETER, SHORTLY AFTER 1600. PINACOTECA VATICANA.

THE APOLLO BELVEDERE, ROMAN COPY OF A GREEK STATUE OF THE FOURTH CENTURY B.C. PIO-CLEMENTINO MUSEUM.

in the progressive attenuation of the sensory data forming his point of departure. Reni was no mystic, but his idealism was the counterpart of the mysticism of the Counter-Reformation and the seventeenth century, sharing its ardent yearnings and, on the whole, its irrationality.

Classicism itself—which is harmony mastered, an equilibrium between the rational and the sensible—became in Reni's hands something equivocal and indefinable. An antique statue, like the *Apollo Belvedere*, might be taken by him in the abstract as a model or a standard. But the model in which the men of the Renaissance recognized themselves was foreign to him; nor could the validity of the standard be checked against a fixed point, a specific rational schema, as it was later by neo-classical artists. Thus Reni's classicism was surrounded, like an object impossible to possess, by a vague halo of eagerness and desire, which imbued it with poetry, though always a generic poetry.

Reni lived through the same times as Caravaggio and, like him, lacked a solid point of reference. Caravaggio was profoundly conscious of this condition and reacted to it dramatically; Reni, on the other hand, drew a veil over it, withdrew into an abstract, aristocratic aloofness, lived out his private dream and nursed a noble illusion.

The two major works executed by Gian Lorenzo Bernini in St Peter's were also designed to oppose and counteract the assertions of the Lutherans. The huge bronze baldachin over the Altar of the Confession marks the spot where St Peter was buried. The vast bronze reliquary in the apse contains, glorifying it as a symbol, the ancient chair on which, according to tradition, the Prince of the Apostles actually sat. The feast of the Chair of St Peter was revived by Pope Paul IV in 1558, at the height of the struggle against Protestantism. The reliquary conceived by Bernini is upheld by statues of two fathers of the Latin Church, St Augustine and St Ambrose, and two of the Greek Church, St Athanasius and St John Chrysostom, together symbolizing the submission of East and West to the Roman See. A huge gilded halo full of angels surmounts the Chair of St Peter, surrounding the luminous window with the dove of the Holy Spirit.

Guido Reni was in the result unsuccessful in his attempt to set himself up against Caravaggio, in the sense in which the Church might have desired—i.e. as a force of certitude against one of doubt, as a positive against a negative pole. Reni's lack of pungency, the ideological vacuum of his work, his graceful charm and undefined reserve had prevented him from taking up and maintaining an official position in this sense. This, however, is precisely what Bernini succeeded in doing. The crisis of the Counter-Reformation was now well on the way to being overcome, as the Church regained full confidence in its ultimate triumph and sought to demonstrate and celebrate its greatness. The echoes of the Protestant heresy were fading away confusedly, drowned out by a lofty hymn: the hymn of the Catholic collectivity.

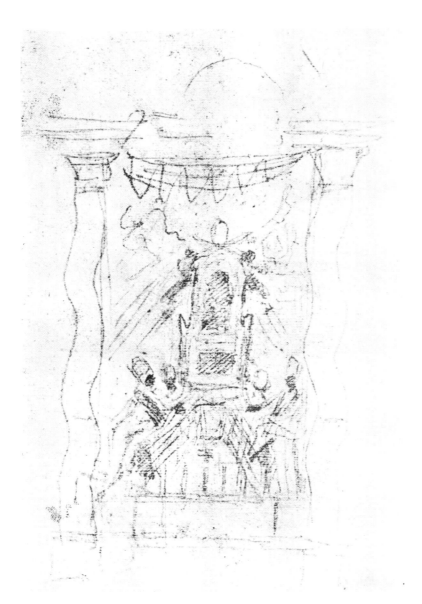

GIAN LORENZO BERNINI (1598-1680):
PRELIMINARY SKETCHES FOR THE RELIQUARY WITH THE CHAIR OF ST PETER.

The Baroque magniloquence of Bernini's style has this demonstrative efficacy, conveys this spell-binding enthusiasm, foments this collective suggestion. Ideologically, then, it succeeds in reconciling the new mystical aspirations, which it delivered from the timorous contrition of the Counter-Reformation, with the Copernican conception of the universe and with the philosophy of the day. What it did, in other words, was to introduce religion anew into a more optimistic and also more vitally contemporary movement of thought; it went far towards retrieving a sense of compelling modernity after the inhibitions, suspected of reaction, under which the philosophic thought of the Counter-Reformation had laboured. The really positive element of Bernini's style, deliberately assumed, was the irrational and fantastic. He seems to take over optimistically the principle fearfully applied by Michelangelo in the *Last Judgement:* that bodies immersed in cosmic space are released from the force of gravity. Thus Bernini's figures are swept up in free and incessant movement, in a triumph of shooting lights that exalts faith with exuberant vitality, thereby bringing a generous and glorious God —the reverse of the terrible God worshipped by Michelangelo—directly into communication with the senses of man.

In 1624 Pope Urban VIII commissioned Bernini to raise a large tabernacle or baldachin over the high altar of St Peter's. The work lasted nine years. On June 29, 1633, the feast day of the Apostle, the baldachin was unveiled. Its construction required an enormous quantity of bronze; some was stripped from the sides of Michelangelo's dome and from the beams in the portico of the Pantheon, some was brought from Venice and Leghorn. While the columns are of solid bronze, the crowning was made of wood overlaid with metal strips.

Bernini, who hitherto had worked only as a sculptor, was here confronted with an architectonic problem of extreme delicacy and solved it with all the brilliant inventiveness of genius. The problem consisted in erecting a huge bulky structure in the heart of the basilica. Here he had to reckon with Michelangelo, for his baldachin had to harmonize with the titanic spatial conception of the church and in no way subvert its carefully balanced proportions or cut off the apsidal zone from view. Had Bernini attempted to bring his architecture into a definite, traditionally canonical relation with Michelangelo's space, he would certainly have failed. The beauty and wisdom of his solution lay in avoiding this relationship.

For the traditional ciborium or altar canopy, a fixed and immovable architectonic structure, he substituted the idea of a baldachin conceived as if made of wood and fabrics, in other words as something portable and mobile. The great baldachin seems to have been not so much erected as placed over the Apostle's tomb, as if carried forward by hand in an imaginary procession and there set down. Or it might be supposed to have been lowered down from above; for its spiralling forms seem to strain upward and converge on a point in the infinite, towards and beyond the vertex of the dome. Not constructed, then, but deposited here for a moment eternized in time, as the ostensible wood and fabrics are sublimated in the enduring metaphor of the bronze, while the limits of its forms tend to shade off and dissolve in an indefinite extension.

Michelangelo's dome marks the culmination of an immense space drawn up almost magnetically to a central point and co-ordinated in it. The Baroque space of Bernini, however, has innumerable centres, and the illusively provisional position of the baldachin does not emphasize so much the singleness as the relativity of the chosen centre. Space as thought out by Michelangelo cannot be infinite, because the infinite, which is God, is a transcendental entity and the transcendental is neither conceivable nor knowable. Bernini, rather than thinking it out, records through the senses a space

GIAN LORENZO BERNINI (1598-1680): RELIQUARY WITH THE CHAIR OF ST PETER. BRONZE AND GOLD, 1656-1666. APSE OF ST PETER'S.

GIAN LORENZO BERNINI (1598-1680): BALDACHIN OVER THE HIGH ALTAR OF ST PETER'S. BRONZE AND GOLD, 1624-1633.

GIAN LORENZO BERNINI (1598-1680): ST AUGUSTINE, DETAIL OF THE RELIQUARY WITH THE CHAIR OF ST PETER, 1656-1666.
APSE OF ST PETER'S.

in which his aspiration towards the infinite and the infinite itself meet and merge; his God is transcendent and immanent at once; his space embraces Being and existence.

Bernini thus came to oppose to the plastic masses and chiaroscuro of Michelangelo's architecture a purely pictorial element of light and colour which, without interfering with their structure and articulation, acts on the atmosphere surrounding those masses. It must not be forgotten, moreover, that he also intervened directly in the internal surfaces of Michelangelo's spatial layout, for it was Bernini who designed the decoration of polychrome marbles extending over a large part of the basilica. This decoration gives a mellow pictorial warmth to the interior, creating a vibrant atmosphere eminently suited to the intense colour accents of the gold and bronze baldachin, which seem to melt and dissolve into it.

The aerial architecture of the baldachin also solves the problem of the apse, which remains clearly visible through the lofty twisting columns, though the view of it is subordinated to the scenographic setting of the baldachin itself. The grandiose reliquary encasing the Chair of St Peter, executed by Bernini from 1656 to 1666 and also made of bronze and gold, stands framed in the very angle of vision opened by the baldachin towards the apse and fits in perfectly with its scenographic character. A preliminary sketch by Bernini, showing the Chair through the columns of the baldachin, reveals how keenly he felt the two monuments to form a unified, organic whole within a single perspective—not linear, however (in the sketch, indeed, he contrives to superimpose the two works), but purely aerial and atmospheric perspective, not intended to channel space towards a vanishing-point but rather to suggest a dissolving effect or fade-out.

While the baldachin seems to have been deposited there by an imaginary cortège, terrestrial or celestial, the Chair is actually being carried, as if in procession, and displayed to the faithful by the giant statues (each measuring over sixteen feet in height) of the Fathers of the Church. The shaft of light bursting in through the window brings to mind the fireworks let off above a motionless procession, enveloping in smoke and flashing lights the sacred images slowly swaying over the heads of the crowd.

But the eager and impassioned sweep of Bernini's vision overcame the limitations of realism and attained a superhuman exaltation. Old age intensified his mysticism, so much so that, with an almost poignant ardour and yearning, his *furia* broke free and soared up towards the heights, as if bent on possessing the infinite. In the Chair of St Peter, the Baroque of Bernini reached the climax of its mature phase and found its most fruitful fulfilment. Sculpture here is effectively and substantially integrated into architecture, in a purely scenographic conception. The figures, which in Michelangelo had personified and symbolized latent structural energies, now act as protagonists within the architecture, not personifying the architectonic action so much as assuming its function.

GIAN LORENZO BERNINI (1598-1680): COLONNADE IN ST PETER'S SQUARE, 1656-1665.

DRAWING OF THE FAÇADE OF ST PETER'S WITH THE TWO BELL-TOWERS DESIGNED BY BERNINI.

In 1637 Bernini was commissioned to add two towers to the façade erected thirty-five years before by Carlo Maderna. Bernini designed two graceful bell-towers in two orders, with arches and corner columns, crowned by a spire. The elevation of the towers would have been about 330 feet, if we add their height (180 feet) to that of the façade (the dome is 435 feet high). But the construction of the lefthand tower brought too great a strain to bear, and cracks appeared in the portico of the church; Maderna in his day had attempted a similar experiment and had run into the same trouble. After the death of Urban VIII, Bernini's patron, the tower already erected was pulled down (1646). Innocent X, the successor of Urban VIII, dismissed Bernini and patronized his rival Borromini. In 1655 Innocent X died and was succeeded by Alexander VII, who recalled Bernini and commissioned him to design and build the great colonnade of St Peter's. On August 28, 1656, the pope laid the foundation stone and by 1665 the vast colonnade was virtually finished. For the traditional atrium of the Early Christian basilicas, Bernini substituted an immense open portico, which took the symbolic form of two outspread arms welcoming the faithful to their embrace. Bernini, as a matter of fact, often took inspiration from the human body in the forms and even the proportions of his architecture.

Baroque architecture and sculpture, with their scenographic accent, are particularly well qualified to solve problems of general arrangement in a given setting, and to join up large spatial units, both within buildings, where they tend to develop a dense, continuous, unitary atmosphere, and outside them, opening them up on the available space, with a peculiar fitness to the requirements of town-planning. In the same years in which Bernini gave the interior of St Peter's its definitive aspect by installing the Chair in the apse, he also achieved happy results outside the basilica with his famous colonnade in St Peter's Square, begun in 1656 and virtually completed by 1665.

The mighty Doric columns standing in serried files create a zone of dense chiaroscuro, in a low, deep-toned key, which accentuates by contrast the luminosity of the square and, instead of sharply stressing its limits, dissolves them in shadow. In this way Bernini increases the size of the square inordinately, again throwing round a broad central space a sonorous suggestion of the infinite. The integration of architectonic space and urban space is worked out in entirely new and modern terms: the church opens on the square, which in turn converges, to its whole immense extent, on the monumental backdrop formed by the façade. The church is like a gigantic body stretching forth its arms, enfolding the mass of the faithful and drawing them to its bosom; Michelangelo's dome, in a contemporary drawing directly alluding to the anthropomorphic conception of Bernini's project, forms the head of this body. The structure as a whole can be identified allegorically with a figure in action.

Bernini's project for reordering the façade did not fare so well. In the years between 1607 and 1612 the surviving part of the Constantinian basilica was demolished and Carlo Maderna, whose design had been chosen from a number of competing projects, completed the work begun by Bramante and Michelangelo. By harmonically prolonging the east end of the nave, he reverted to the plan in the form of a Latin cross and, by adding a monumental order of columns to the entrance, achieved a dignified solution to the thorny problem of the façade. When, on Maderna's death (in 1629), Bernini succeeded him as chief architect of St Peter's, he revived a project originally conceived by Maderna himself, who had proposed to erect a tower at each end of the façade in order to break up its uniform horizontal extension. In 1637 Bernini designed the two towers. But hardly had the first been built when cracks and fissures appeared in the portico; after lengthy discussions the whole project was abandoned and in 1646 the tower already erected was pulled down.

These vicissitudes brought to a close the reconstruction of St Peter's, begun a century and a half before, on which now Bernini set the seal of Baroque. He also left his imprint on the papal residence, transforming the entrance ramp, with an extraordinary orchestration of light and shadow effects, into a large and magnificent staircase: the Scala Regia or main stairs (1663-1666). This work too comes under the heading of architecture, in its tension and movement, so nobly and harmoniously vibrant.

GIAN LORENZO BERNINI (1598-1680): THE SCALA REGIA, OR GRAND STAIRCASE, IN THE VATICAN PALACE, 1663-1666.

ANTONIO CANOVA (1757-1822): CLEMENT XIII PRAYING, DETAIL OF THE TOMB OF POPE CLEMENT XIII, 1784-1792. NORTH TRANSEPT OF ST PETER'S.

The seventeenth century then, Baroque and theatrical, attained its triumphant fulfilment in the new St Peter's. The neo-classical style, which forms the transition from the last decades of the eighteenth century to the early decades of the nineteenth, gives in its clear harmonies a lucid reflection of the Age of Enlightenment, in which the ideal and the beautiful already verge upon the rational in the modern sense; and it was this style that governed the creation and arrangement of the Vatican Museums. The idea of the Beautiful, which Winckelmann, the theorist of neo-classicism, identified with the *Apollo Belvedere*, was no longer for the neo-classicists, as it had been for Guido Reni, something vague and unattainable; it had crystallized into something concrete and definite. The *Apollo Belvedere* is not an original Greek statue; it is a rather poor and schematic copy. But in its very schematism it assumed for the neo-classicists a symbolic and programmatic character: it was the proportions of the statue that fascinated the new artists and inspired the rational criteria of physical beauty which they adopted.

Clement XIII (1758-1769), the pope who beside the Museo Sacro founded by Benedict XIV installed the Museo Profano and appointed Winckelmann Prefect of Antiquities in Rome, is portrayed on his marble tomb in an attitude of patient and meditative humility. Clement was a pope who already belonged to the new times—sadder times for the papacy, certainly less glorious and inspiring, and harder times too for Italian art. The author of this portrait is Canova, the major Italian representative of Neo-Classicism; but it cannot be said that, by way of his neo-classical ideal, Canova has resolved the incongruities of his personality. He remains committed, on the one hand, to a full-flavoured, anecdotal, illustrative vein which owes much to the racy Goldonian wit and vivacity of the Venice of his youth, and which, already in this sculpture, heralds the good-natured verism of the early nineteenth century; on the other hand, his work comes as a vague and plaintive echo of seventeenth century sensualism, which prevents him from defining his style in terms of the new ideals with the same clarity that in France determined the vision of a David.

With Canova, Italian art withdraws from the European scene, where for centuries it had played a leading role, and recedes now into the shadows of nineteenth century provincialism. Its past glories were henceforth to be enshrined in the great museums of Europe. Of these, the Vatican collections, owing not only to their incomparable wealth but also to the historic settings of the galleries housing them, rank as one of the greatest and most suggestive.

BIBLIOGRAPHICAL GUIDE

GENERAL INDEX

LIST OF ILLUSTRATIONS

BIBLIOGRAPHICAL GUIDE

TO THE WORKS REFERRED TO IN THE TEXT

ARGAN, Giulio Carlo, *Fra Angelico*, Geneva 1955.

BAGLIONE, Giovanni, *Le vite de' pittori, scultori, architetti ed intagliatori*, Rome 1642.

BATTISTI, Eugenio, *Giotto*, Geneva 1960.

BELLORI, Giovanni Pietro, *Le vite de' pittori, scultori ed architetti moderni*, Rome 1672.

BURCKHARDT, Jacob, *Der Cicerone: eine Anleitung zum Genuss der Kunstwerke Italiens*, Leipzig 1928 (first published 1855); English translation of the sections relating to painting by Mrs A. H. Clough, London 1873.

CAMPOS, Deoclecio Redig de, *Sopra una tavola sconosciuta del secolo XI rappresentante il Giudizio Universale*, in *Rendiconti della Pontifica Accademia Romana di Archeologia*, XI, 1935, pp. 139-156.

CAMPOS, Deoclecio Redig de, *Itinerario pittorico dei Musei Vaticani*, Rome 1954.

CIAMPINI, Giovanni, *De sacris aedificiis a Constantino Magno constructis*, Rome 1693.

CONDIVI, Ascanio, *Vita di Michelangelo*, Rome 1553.

FRIEDLÄNDER, Walter, *Caravaggio Studies*, Princeton 1955.

GREGOROVIUS, Ferdinand, *Geschichte der Stadt Rom im Mittelalter*, Stuttgart 1859-1872; English translation by A. Hamilton, London 1894-1900.

GNUDI, Cesare, *Giotto*, Milan 1958.

LEONARDO DA VINCI, *Trattato della Pittura*, first edition, Paris 1651; translated and annotated by A. Philip McMahon, with an introduction by Ludwig H. Heydenreich, Princeton 1956.

MARTINELLI, Valentino, *Donatello e Michelozzo a Roma*, in *Commentari*, VIII, 1957, pp. 167-194.

PANOFSKY, Erwin, *Die Perspektive als symbolische Form*, in *Vorträge der Bibliothek Warburg, Vorträge 1924-1925*, Leipzig-Berlin 1927.

RANKE, Leopold von, *Die römischen Päpste in den letzten vier Jahrhunderten*, Berlin 1834-1839; *History of the Popes*, London 1878.

TOLNAY, Charles de, *Michelangelo*, Vol. II, *The Sistine Ceiling*, Princeton 1945, and Vol. V, *The Final Period*, Princeton 1960; *Michelangelo*, Florence 1951.

TORRIGGIO, Francesco Maria, *Le Sacre Grotte Vaticane*, Viterbo 1618.

VASARI, Giorgio, *Le vite de' piu eccellenti architetti, pittori et scultori italiani*, first edition, Florence 1550; second edition, Florence 1568; *Lives of the Most Eminent Painters, Sculptors and Architects*, translated by Gaston du C. de Vere, London 1912-1915.

VEGIO, Maffeo, *De rebus antiquis memorabilibus basilicae S. Petri*.

VENTURI, Adolfo, *Storia dell'Arte Italiana*, Vol. IV, *La Scultura del Trecento*, Milan 1905.

VENTURI, Lionello, *La data dell'attività romana di Giotto*, in *L'Arte*, XXI, 1918, pp. 229-235.

VESPASIANO DA BISTICCI, *Vita di uomini del secolo XV*, Bologna 1892; *The Vespasiano Memoirs, Lives of Illustrious Men of the XVth Century*, translated by William George and Emily Waters, London 1926.

WICKHOFF, Franz, *Die bronzene Apostelstatue in der Peterskirche*, in *Zeitschrift für bildende Kunst*, I, 1890, pp. 108-114.

GENERAL INDEX

LIST OF ILLUSTRATIONS

CHAPTER 4

213

CHAPTER 5

PRINTED BY
IRL IMPRIMERIES RÉUNIES LAUSANNE S.A.

PRINTED IN SWITZERLAND